Anonymous

History of India

Part 3

Anonymous

History of India
Part 3

ISBN/EAN: 9783337820886

Printed in Europe, USA, Canada, Australia, Japan

Cover: Foto ©ninafisch / pixelio.de

More available books at **www.hansebooks.com**

THE
HISTORY OF INDIA

As Told By Its Own Historians

THE MUHAMMADAN PERIOD

THE POSTHUMOUS PAPERS

OF THE LATE

SIR H. M. ELLIOT

Edited by Prof. John Dowson

PUBLISHERS' NOTE

The present volume, like its predecessor, is made up of twenty-five articles which appeared in the Eighth Volume of the original edition of this work and which saw the light of day in 1877.

As numerous short articles were published in the said volume, the Editor says it is "not possible to give a complete list of the translators." As far as he could ascertain, he gives the names of the translators of a few of the articles the list of which is given below:

1. *Tarikh-i Shahadat-i Farrukh Siyar*—Editor.
2. *'Ibrat Nama*—Editor.
3. *Tarikh-i Ibrahim Khan*—Major Fuller.
4. *Gul-i Rahmat*—Editor.

CONTENTS

		PAGE
1.	Farhatu-n Nazirin	9
2.	Reign of Alamgir II	14
3.	Tarikh-i Faiz Bakhsh	21
4.	Hadikatu-l Akalim	26
5.	Jam-i Jahan-Numa	29
6.	Ma-Asiru-l Umara	31
7.	Tazkiratu-l Umara	37
8.	Sawanih-i Akbari	37
9.	Siyaru-l Mula-akhkhirin	38
10.	Mulakhkhasu-t Tawarikh	43
11.	Tarikh-i Mamalik-i Hind	44
12.	Chahar Gulzar Shuja'i	47
13.	Death of 'Aliwardi Khan	54
14.	Tarikh-i Shahadat-i Farrukh Siyar	76
15.	Waki'at-i Azfari	79
16.	Bahru-l Mawwaj	79
17.	'Ibrat-Nama	81
18.	Martyrdom of Alamgir II	86
19.	Chahar Gulshan	100
20.	Tarikh-i Ibrahim Khan	101
21.	Origin and Genealogy of the Mahrattas	102
22.	Lubbu-s Siyar	143
23.	Ausaf-i Asaf	146
24.	Tarikh of Jugal Kishwar	146
25.	Gulistan-i Rahmat	146
26.	Shah-nama, or Munawwaru-l Kalan	159
27.	Ikhtisaru-t Tawarikh	160
28.	Mir-at-i Aftab-numa	160

IMPORTANT CORRECTION

After page 56 please treat the pages 49—64 in the fourth formé as 57 to 72. These page numbers are obvious misprints.

STUDIES IN INDIAN HISTORY
PART III

FARHATU-N NAZIRIN
OF
MUHAMMAD ASLAM

A GENERAL History of India, composed by Muhammad Aslam, son of Muhammad Hafizu-l Ansari, and concluded in the year 1184 A.H. (1770-1 A.D.).

This History is somewhat ambitious in style, but of no great value for its contents. The author informs us in his Preface that, "in the bloom of his youth, when he was yet a student, in the city of Lucknow (may God preserve it!), the heavenly inspirer whispered several times in the ear of this meanest person of mankind as follows:—'O thou who art the painter of the various scenes of the gallery of the world, and the describer of the works of Nature! Since to thank and praise those who are the worshippers of God is in fact to thank and praise the Almighty Creator Himself, it is proper that thou shouldst compile a work, comprising the history of the Prophets, the Imams, the Muhammadan Emperors, and the religious and learned men, by whose holy exertions the management of the country of Hindustan has been invisibly supported."

"Independent of this divine afflatus, he mentions other reasons which induced him to devote his attention to history—such as the universal desire to read historical works, combined with the exceeding difficulty of procuring them; the eagerness to acquire a knowledge of the manners and customs of the ancients, of the accounts of travellers, biographies of famous persons, and of the wonders of the world. In order to satisfy this general curiosity, he early accustomed himself to make extracts from books of travels and historical works, in order to compile a "history which might contain the most important and interesting matters, and which form its lucid and methodical construction and exceeding comeliness, might meet the approbation of the most enlightened minds. But as 'all works must be performed at the time destined for them,' the task was delayed till he had completed his studies."

After he had been fully educated, he visited the city of Faizabad in A.H. 1182, where he met the "most puissant and exalted Nazim Jang Mudabbiru-l Mulk Rafi'u-d daula Monsieur Gentil, and petitioned through his intercession for his livelihood in the most high court of the world-benefiting and noble *wazir* of Hindustan, whose praise is beyond all expression. That light of the edifice of greatness and the sun of dignity showed him great kindness, and said that he himself was fond of knowledge, and always devoted himself to the study of histories. It was therefore desirable that the author should take pains to write a most interesting account of the *wazir's* noble family, of the Emperors of Hindustan, the Prophets and the eminently religious and learned men; to make the horse of his pen gallop over the field of eloquence, and like a diver bring out from the ocean of his mind such shining pearls as might adorn Hindustan with their light, and be ornaments to the ear of curiosity. Prepare, said he, such a rose-bower as may echo with the songs of the nightingales of the garden of knowledge."

Under these happy auspices, he commenced to labour in collecting the histories of Hindustan, and obtained from different places a great number of authentic works —such as the *Tarikh-i Nizamu-d din Ahmad Bakhshi, Mirat-i 'Alam,* and Firishta. He also informs us that he carefully persued other books, such as the *Tarikh-i Bahmani, Taju-l Ma-asir, Tarjuma Yamini, Tarikh-i Firoz Shahi, Tarikh-i Alfi, Habi-bu-s Siyar, Rauzatu-s Safa, Timur-nama, Waki'at-i Babari. Waki'at-i Humayuni, Akbar-nama, Shah Jahan-nama, 'Alamgir-nama, Tarikh-i Bahadur Shah,* etc. "He made abstracts of these treasures, which like scattered pearls were separate from each other, and strung them upon one thread after a peculiar plan, to be remembered by posterity, in this charming garden, which is entitled *Farhatu-n Nazirin*, the 'Delight of Observers.' "

The author states that he wrote his Preface in the year 1184 A.H. (1770 A.D.), and dedicated the work to the "most prudent *wazir*, the gem of the mine of liberality, of most noble extraction, the select of the whole creation, the leader of the army of victory, Shuja'u-d daula Bahadur, in the hope that he would approve of it, and that it might go forth like the wind to the different quarters of the earth, and like unadulterated coin might obtain circulation throughout all countries. The readers of this mirror of the world are requested to consider the little leisure he had from his other avocations, and to remove with the sleeve of kindness the dust of inaccuracy which might soil its splendour, and to spare their reproaches."

The auuthor divides his work into an Introduction, three Books, and a Conclusion; but the latter, which is said to contain "an account of the Prime Minister and the learned and religious of *that* (his) time," is not contained in the volume I have examined, which ends with a promise to write more concerning the Prime Minister, whose praises he is sounding. The Paris copy is also deficient in this Conclusion, but both contain an account of the famous men of Aurangzeb's time at the close of his reign; but no other reign, either before or after it, has any biographical notice of contemporaries.

CONTENTS

Preface, pp. 1 to 17—Introduction, The Creation, pp. 17 to 20—Book I. Prophets, Patriarchs, Muhammad and Imams, pp. 20 to 122—Book II. The Rajas and Sultans of India, from the time of Ham, pp. 123 to 170—Book III. Timur and the Timurian Dynasty, to the twelfth year of Shah 'Alam's reign, pp. 171 to 520.

The *Farhatu-n Nazirin* is very rare in India. I know of only one copy, and that is in the possession of Nawab Taki Khan of Rohilkhand. From the numerous erasures and interlineations I should judge it to be an autograph. There is also a copy in England which was available to Dr. Lee, for he quotes it at p. 130 of his translation of the *Travels of Ibn Batuta*, but he does not notice it in his Preface, where he describes the other works which he quotes, nor does he mention the Library in which it is to be found. There is a copy in the British Museum, No. 6942, and one also in the Royal Library at Paris (Fonds Gentil 47, small folio of 1022 pages, of 17 lines each). SIZE—Large 8vo., pages of 19 lines in each, closely written.

EXTRACTS

In the third year of Ahmad Shah's reign, corresponding with A.H. 1160, Ahmad Shah Durrani, with the renewed intention of conquering Hindustan, arrived in the neighbourhood of Sodra, and Mir Mu'inu-l Mulk, *alias* Mir Mannu, left Lahore with an army for the purpose of expelling him; but, being unable to take the field against him, he intrenched himself. The nobles and *mirzas* of Dehli hoped that Mir Mannu might be destroyed, and after this desirable event they would take measures against the Abdali. They would thus extirpate the thorn which the race of the Turanis had planted in their side. The Mir requested assistance from the Emperor of Dehli and his minister for four months, but all in vain. He was consequently obliged to sue for peace, and he persuaded the Durrani to return to Kandahar by assigning to him four *mahals,* viz. Sailkot, Pasrur, Gujarat, and Aurangabad, which had belonged to Kabul from the time of Alamgir.[1] The Durrani, having reached Kandhar, collected a large force, and returned with the intention of conquering Hindustan.

In 1164 A.H. (1750-1 A.D.) Ahmad came by forced marches to Lahore, and began to devastate the country. In the month of Rabi'u-l awwal he crossed the Chinab,

---

[1] Compare Cunningham's *History of the Sikhs*, p. 102.

and encamped between Sodra and Wazirabad. Mu'inu-l Mulk also, at the head of a formidable army, crossed the Ravi, which flows under the city of Lahore, and pitched his tents in front of the invader. For some time there was continued firing with guns and matchlocks, and the whole country between the Ravi and Chinab was desolated by the ravages and massacres committed by the Durranis. In those days the writer of these leaves was engaged in learning the Kuran by heart. In the end, neither party gained any perceptible advantage. The Durranis suddenly broke up their quarters, with the intention of crossing the Ravi, and plundering the district and city of Lahore. Mir Mannu marched back in alarm to the city, barricaded all the streets, and strengthened the interior defences. Every day there were skrimishes, till at last the supply of provisions was closed on all sides. There was such a dearth of corn and grass that with the utmost difficulty two *sirs* of wheat flour could be had for a rupee, to say nothing of rice. To procure for horses other forage than rushes or house-thatch was next to an impossibility. This obliged Mir Mannu and his army to take the field. He sallied out with his right and left wings, and fanned the embers of war into a flame. The chief agent of Mir Mannu was a man named Koral Mal, who had been corn-chandler, and could scarcely earn his bread, but had now become master of immense riches, and had obtained kettle-drums and flags, with the governorship of Multan. With him, Adina Beg Khan Bahram Jang[2] had for certain reasons

[2][*This Adina or Dina Beg Khan, whose name will frequently recur in these pages, was by caste an Arain, and son of a man named Channu, an inhabitant of the village of Sarakpur, near Lahore. He was brought up in a Mughal family, and in early life spent a good deal of his time at Allahabad, Kanpore, and Bajwara. He became a soldier, but seems to have thrown aside that profession for revenue work. He was an able man and*

taken some cause of offence, and retired to his own government in the (Jalandhar) Doab. Adina Beg now reluctantly joined Mu'inu-l Mulk against the Durranis, and, availing himself of his opportunity in the midst of battle, instructed one of the Afghans of Kusur to put an end to the existence of that unworthy wretch Kora Mal by a musket-ball.[2] In consequence of his death, the army of Mir Mannu suffered a complete defeat, and he was obliged to send for his horse, and, advancing with some of his personal attendants, proceeded to kiss the threshold of the Durrani, who honoured him with the grant of a valuable *khila'at* and the title of *Farzand Khan*.

Reign of 'Alamgir II

In the third year of the reign of 'Alamgir II., the minister Ghaziu-d din Khan, having released Wala Gauhar, the eldest son of 'Alimgir, from prison, took him towards

a good accountant, and he began as collector of the village of Kanak near Ludhiyana, from which humble position he advanced till he was made Governor of Sultanpur, an office which he held at the time of Nadir Shah's invasion. He died without heirs at Khanpur near Hoshiyarpur, where a fine tomb was erected over his remains. These particulars are extracted from a little work called "Ahwal Adina Beg Khan, which is of course eulogistic, but the stories it tells of him show that he was shrewd, artful, unscrupulous and sometimes cruel, as when he condemned a confectioner, who had declined to supply him with preserves, to be boiled alive, "as he boiled his own jam." The poor wretch was saved by the intercession of Adina's guests, but "felt a burning pain in his body ever afterwards." Boiling or half boiling, seems to have been a torture in use at this period.]

[2] *This is opposed to the common account, which represents Kora Mal as killed honourably in action. See Prinsep's Ranjeet Singh, p. 12, and Cunningham's Hist. of the Sikhs, p. 103.*

Lahore. He went as far as Ludhiyana, and then returned, and having sent for the daughter of Mu'inu-l Mulk from Lahore, he married her. He deprived the Emperor of all power whatever, and conducted all the affairs of the State. A misunderstanding arose during this year between him and Najibu-d daula, which at this very day is the cause of all the disorganization which is ruining the country.

Najibu-d daula, having found means of secretly communicating with the Abdali, invited him to come to Hindustan. Accordingly, in the beginning of the fouth year of the reign, he came to Dehli, and, having ravaged it, proceeded to Mattra, where he massacred the inhabitants, broke the temples, and having plundered the town of immense wealth in property and cash, he cut the very nose of Hindustan, and returned to Lahore, where he gave his youngest son the title of Timur Shah; and left Jahan Khan there with the designation of minister. *Waziru-l mamalik* Ghaziu-d din Khan marched his army into the provinces of Allahabad and Oudh, but returned to Dehli without meeting with any success. Najib Khan and Kutb Shah, having collected a force, plundered the house of Ghaziu-d din Khan, carried off all the cash, furniture and jewels which were found in it, and also dishonoured his *zenana*. Ghaziu-d din, assembling a body of men, sat watching the opportunity of vengeance, but in vain.

Adina Beg Khan, being sorely pressed by the army of the Abdalis, invited Malhar, Raghu and other Mahratta chiefs from the Dakhin, gave them fifty *lacs* of rupees, and proceeded to attack the officers of the Abdali. He first overcame the *Faujdar* of Sirhind,[a] whose name was 'Abdu-s Samad Khan, and who was stationed in that city with a body of 20,000 Rohillas, horse and foot. After subjugating the whole of that district, Adina Beg proceeded to Lahore. When he reached that city, Jahan

---

[a] *The author writes it Shaharind.*

Khan, with Prince Timur, pitched his tents at Karachi-sarai, and having intrenched himself, prepared for action. Adina Beg Khan joined his forces with those of the Mahrattas, and Jahan Khan, having sustained a defeat, fled towards Peshwar with two hundred horse, leaving all his treasure and property to be plundered by the enemy's army.

Adina Beg Khan, on the achievement of this unexpected victory, ordered the happy occasion to be celebrated by beat of drums. He dismissed the Mahratta army to Dehli, and himself proceeded to Batala, where he fixed his head-quarters. He then turned his attention to the appointment of governors for the provinces of Multan, Thatta, and Lahore. Soon after this he died a natural death, on the 11th of Muharram, in the fifth year of 'Alamgir's reign, and the province of Lahore again came into the possession of the Sikhs.

Ghaziu-d din Khan sent Jhanku Mahratta against Najibu-d daula, who, being unable to oppose him, departed to Sakartal on the banks of the Ganges, where he fixed his batteries, and prepared for resistance. He sent his envoy to Ahmad Shah Abdali to solicit assistance. The army of Jhanku invested him closely, and after four months' fighting, it crossed the Ganges near Hardwar, where the river was found fordable, and overran the country. Nawab Shuja'u-d daula, son of Waziru-l mamalik Mansuru-l Mulk Safdar Jang, who was coming to aid Najibu-d daula, arrived soon after, and expelled the Mahrattas from the territory of the Afghans. Ghaziu-d din Khan, on receiving the news of Shuja'u-d daula's arrival, marched from Dehli and joined the camp of Jhanku. He then directed some of his sardars to go to the fort of Shah-Jahanabad, and put 'Azizu-d din ('Alamgir) to death.

In the mean time Ahmad Shah Abdali reached the environs of Sirhind, and defeated the Mahratta army which was quartered in that district. On receiving the intelligence, Jhanku advanced to oppose the Abdali.

Najib Khan, finding an opportunity, joined the Abdali's camp at Saharanpur, by forced marches. Jhanku, having sustained a repulse at that place, came to Dehli, where he fought a very severe battle, but was at last obliged to fly.

The period of 'Alamgir the Second's reign is said to be six years, and that of his life about sixty. The events above related took place in A.H. 1174 (1760-1 A.D.).

I will minutely relate the Abdali's victory over the Dakhin army, when we enter upon his history in detail. I content myself here with giving a concise narrative of it as follows. When Jhanku sustained a defeat from the army of the Abdali, and fled away with Ghaziu-d din Khan, the Abdali sacked Dehli and encamped at Anupnagar. Shuja'u-d daula also came there and kissed his threshold. After the rainy season, Bhao Wiswas Rai, with the son of the Raja his master, marched from the Dakhin at the head of 200,000 horse, 20,000 foot, and 300 guns. He entered the city of Dehli, and having taken the fort from the officers of the Abdali, proceeded to Kunjpura and Sirhind. 'Abdu-s Samad Khan and seven other officers who were stationed at the former place, with a body of 20,000 horse and foot, offered resistance, and after a battle of about one hour, were all slain. Bhao plundered Kunjpura, sent those who were taken alive to prison, and pitched his tents on the banks of the Jumna.

Ahmad Shah, on hearing this sad news, writhed like a serpent, and kindling the fire of anger, moved towards the enemy. Although the river flowed with great impetuosity, yet he forded it at Baghpat, and engaged with the enemy, who, not being able to withstand him in the field, retreated to Panipat, and fixed their batteries there. The Abdali besieged their camp, and when the siege had lasted five months, the enemy one morning left their intrenchments, and drew out their army in battle array. The fire of battle raged from early morn and was not extinguished till evening. At last the gale of victory blew over the royal flags, and all the Dakhin host was cut down by the swords of the Muhammadan warriors. Of their chiefs none except Malhar saved his life. The dead lay strewn shoulder to shoulder from the plain of Panipat to Dehli. About ninety thousand persons, male and female, were taken prisoners, and obtained eternal happiness by embracing the Muhammadan faith. Indeed, never was such a splendid victory achieved from the time of Amir Mahmud Subuktigin to the present day by any of the Sultans but by this Emperor of Emperors. After this conquest, he appointed Waziru-l mamalik Shuja'uld daula to the office of *Wazir*, Najib Khan to that of *Bakhshi*, and having granted tracts of land to the other Afghans, and dismissed them to their respective abodes, returned himself to Kandahar.

The history of this sovereign is given in full detail in its proper place.

When Nawab Shuja'u-d daula arrived in his province, he went to kiss the threshold of His Majesty Wala Gauhar Shah 'Alam, and obtained the high rank of Prime Minister. I am now going to relate a full account of this great Emperor and his wise Minister.

Shah 'Alam, son of 'Alamgir the Second

That prince of noble extraction, the jewel of the crown of sovereignty, fought a battle with Ghaziu-d din Khan in the fifth year of his venerable father's reign, and having left Dehli, proceeded to the eastward. None of the Afghan chiefs received him hospitably, through fear of Ghaziu-d din Khan. He was obliged to resort to that hero of the world (Shuja'u-d daula) in the fort of Jalalabad, where he was respectfully and hospitably received. After some days' halt, he proceeded to invade Bengal. Muhammad Kuli Khan, Governor of the province of Allahabad, and Zainu-l 'Abidin Khan, joined him. He allowed them to remain with the camp, and ordered them to raise an army.

In a few days a force of about one hundred thousand

horsemen was collected, and he went to take Patna 'Azimabad. After the city was besieged, and much blood was shed, Miran, son of Ja'far 'Ali Khan, Governor of the province of Bengal, assembled a large force, and having invited the Firingi armies to assist him, waged war with the Emperor. Though the garrison was on the point of being overpowered and Miran of taking to flight, yet, through the disaffection of the nobles in whom the Emperor confided, and the want of treasure, which can never be amassed without possessing dominion (dominion and treasure being twins), great disaffection arose in the Emperor's army. Many, from fear of scarcity of provisions, went to their homes, and others who had no shame joined with Ram Narain and Miran The army of the Emperor met with a terrible defeat. Just afterwards Miran was killed by a stroke of lightning, and peace was concluded by the agency of the Christians

Muhammad Kuli Khan came to Allahabad and the news of 'Azizu-d din 'Alamgir's death reached Shah 'Alam in Patna. on which he was much afflicted in his mind; but ascribing the event to the wise dispensations of Providence, he sat upon the throne of sovereignty on the 5th of Jumada-l awwal. Nawab Shuja'u-d daula, after a few days, came to the border of his territories, and having invited the Emperor from 'Azimabad, obtained the honour of an interview, and was exalted to the hereditary office of *Wazir*, and afterwards accompanied him to Allahabad. It is through the means of that great man that the name of Sahib Kiran Gurgan (Timur) still remains; otherwise, the Abdali would not have allowed one of his descendants to survive.

The Emperor now fixed his residence at Allahabad, kept the eldest son of Shuja'u-d daula in his Court as deputy of his father, whom he permitted to return to the province of Oudh, which is his *jagir* and *tuyūghā*: As it is at this time the 1180th year of the Hijra,[5] it is

[5]*There is an error here*—1184 A.H. (1770 A.D.) *is meant.*

therefore the twelfth year of His Majesty's reign, which commenced from the month of Jumada-l awwal. May God render His Majesty kind towards all wise and learned men, towards the poor, and towards all his subjects: and may he give him grace to walk in the paths of the Holy Law!

To relate in detail the events of Shah 'Alam's reign would require a separate history. The writer contents himself therefore with giving the above succinct account of him.

Nawabs of Oudh

Burhanu-l Mulk, in consideration of the valuable services he had rendered to the Emperor, was elevated to the rank of five thousand personal and the command of five thousand horse. He also obtained the title of *Bahadur Jang* and the governorship of Agra; and greatly exerted himself in subverting and destroying the rebels. When Maharaja Jai Singh Sawai was sent against Churaman Jat, the governorship of the province of Oudh was conferred on Burhanu-l Mulk, and with it that title. He took such measures that no trace of revolters remained within the limits of his province. This is well known and requires no comment.

At the time of the invasion of Nadir Shah, he came to Court with all haste, and although dissuaded by the Emperor and the nobles, yet he fought very boldly against the Shah. After the action he visited the Shah, and was received with great honour. Distressed beyond measure at the misfortunes which afflicted the times, he poisoned himself,[a] leaving Safdar Jang Abu-l Mansur Khan, his sister's son, as his successor, in whose forehead the light

---

[a] *The Ma-asiru-l umara says he died of his wounds. Dow (vol. ii. p. 425) gives a romantic account of his being induced to poison himself through Asaf Jah's duplicity. The Siyaru-l Muta-akhkhirin says he died of a mortification in the foot (Briggs, vol. i. p. 429).*

of greatness shone, and in whose appearance the marks of dignity and grandeur were conspicious. At the time of the invasion of Ahmad Shah Abdali, who killed Nadir Shah, and had come down with a numerous army to conquer Hindustan, Safdar Jang, with great intrepidity, stood firm to his ground, and, with a view to preserve his honour and fame, fought very severe battles with that hardy and stubborn enemy. Although Kamru-d-din Khan, the minister, had fallen, and the son of Raja Jai Singh Sawai had fled from the field; although at the same time the news of the death of the Emperor was received, and the royal army was routed and dispressed, yet he repulsed and defeated him. After the flight of the Abdali, he placed Ahmad Shah upon the throne, and, assuming the office of *wazir*, brought him to Dehli, and turned his attention to the administration of the Government. As at all times the creators of disturbance were at their work, a misunderstanding arose between him and the Emperor. For some time he was engaged in punishing and subduing the insurgents, and tried to correct the conduct of the Emperor, who, being addicted to luxury and pleasure, took no care of his duties.¹ But seeing that it was all in vain, he left the Emperor, and went to the province which had been assigned to him. After some days he expired, and was succeeded by his son, the most upright, accomplished, and brave Jalalu-d din Haidar Shuja'u-d daula, who in the time of Shah 'Alam obtained the office of *wazir*, and excelled all competitors in wealth and rank. The son was even superior to the father, and an account of him is given elsewhere.

TARIKH-I FAIZ BAKHSH
OF
SHEO PARSHAD

This is a history of the Afghans of Rohilkhand, and details the transactions between them and the Nawabs of

---

¹*See the admirable letter of remonstrance addressed*

Oudh with such copiousness as to render it worth translation. It was compiled at the desire of General Kirkpatrick in A.H. 1190 (A.D. 1776), by Sheo Parshad, who gives the following account of the reasons which induced him to undertake the task. He says that one day in camp, between Bilgram and Mallawan, he was introduced in Colonel Collins's tent by Captain Keelpatrick (?) to his brother (General ?) Kirkpatrick, who had lately arrived from Chunar, and the author was so much pleased with his affability and condescension, that he offered his services to that officer, who desired him to give an account of the Afghans of Katehr, from the time of Nawab 'Ali Muhammad Khan, when they first acquired power, to the affair of Laldong, in order that he might translate it into English, and forward it to the King of England (Farang). When he returned to the tent, he had a sleepless night; and he declares that if he were to tell all the thoughts which occupied and distracted his mind during that night, a volume would not suffice. Finding on the morrow that General Kirkpatrick was not able fully to comprehend his verbal history, he determined upon writing it, in order that that gentleman might at his leisure translate it with the aid of his *munshi*. He accordingly set to work to compose his narrative, and finished it in March, A.D. 1776.

The history by Faiz Bakhsh, of Faizabad, is also known by the name of *Tarikh-i Faiz Bakhsh;* and as both of them treat of the same period, there is great probability of confounding the two works. The work, though written by a Hindu, not only opens with the usual laud of the Deity, but proceeds to celebrate Muhammad, and the Chahar Yar besides.

SIZE—8vo., 388 pages of 13 lines each.

CONTENTS

Praise of God, the Prophet, and his four friends—
to him by *Nizamu-l Mulk, Asiatic Miscellany*, vol. i. p. 482.

Account of Nawab Faizu-llah Khan—City of Rampur—
The Kosi river—Introduction—Arrival of the Afghans,
and an account of the Katchr territory—Shah 'Alam
Khan and Hasan Khan's arrival in Katchr—Shah 'Alam
Khan—Rise of Nawab Muhammad Khan—The eunuch
defeated and slain—Saifu-d din routed and killed—
Defeat and death of Raja Barnard Khattri—Defeat of
the Raja and conquest of the Kamaun hills—Arrival of
Muhammad Shah at Bangash—Nawab 'Ali Muhammad
Khan returns to Katchr from Sirhind—Nawab Kamru-d
din Khan killed—Death of the Emperor Muhammad
Shah—Nawab 'Ali Muhammad Khan takes possession of
the whole territory of Katchr—Death of Nawab 'Ali
Muhammad Khan—Kutbu-d din Khan' slain—Kaim
Jang slain—Arrival of Safdar Jang to seize Kaim Jang's
property—Rise of Nawab Ahmad Khan Bangash, and
death of Raja Nuwul Rai—Defeat of Safdar Jang—
Nawab Sa'du-llah Khan proceeds to aid Ahmad Khan
Bangash—Ahmad Khan defeated by Safdar Jang, and
taken prisoner in the forest of Jalkana—Wealth and
luxury of Najib Khan—Settlement of matters with
Safdar Jang—Nawab 'Abdu-llah Khan's return from
Kandahar to Katchr—Differences between 'Abdu-llah
Khan, Faizu-llah Khan, Sa'du-llah Khan, and other
Nawabs—'Abdu-llah Khan's animosity against Nawab
Faizu-llah Khan—Arrival of Nawab 'Abdu-llah Khan
and others in Katchr, and allowances made to them—
Allowances fixed for the author's master and Nawab
Sa'du-llah Khan—Death of Murtaza Khan—Death of
Allah Yar Khan—Power gained by Safdar Jang—Jawed
Khan killed by Safdar Jang—Ahmad Shah is disgusted
with Safdar Jang—Nawab Sa'adat Khan revolts at the
instigation of Safdar Jang—Rebellion of Safdar Jang and
the battle which ensued—Disagreement between Zu-l
fikar Jang and Nawab Safdar Jang—Suraj Mal Jat taken
prisoner by 'Imadu-l Mulk—Capture of Ahmad Shah—
Ascension of 'Aziz-ud din 'Alamgir Badshah to the throne
—Daughter of Nawab Mu'inu-l Mulk brought from

Lahore—Celebration of her marriage—Exchange of turbans between Nawab Shuja'u-d daula and Sa'du-llah Khan—Nawab 'Imadu-l Mulk comes to expel Shuja'u-d daula from the estate of the sons of Nawab Faizu-llah Khan—Nawab Ja'far 'Ali Khan and Khan 'Ali Khan's friendship with Sa'du-llah Khan—Janku and other Dakhin chiefs come against Najibu-d daula—Shuja'u-d daula with the nobility of Katehr proceeds to assist him—Ahmad Shah comes from Kandahar to aid Najibu-d daula—The chiefs of Katehr join the camp of Ahmad Shah Durrani—Bhao and other chiefs of the Dakhin come to fight with the Durrani King—The Dakhin chiefs are deserted by Suraj Mal Jat; they proceed to Panipat; Kutb Shah and Mumin Khan are slain—Ahmad Shah marches from Anupshahr to punish the Dakhin chiefs—Nawab Faizu-llah Khan reaches the camp of the King, and joins with him in the crusade—Bhao and other Dakhin chiefs slain—The Emperor returns to Dehli—He takes Suraj Mal Jat into his favour, and confirms him in his possessions—The Doab districts granted to the chiefs of Katehr—'Imadu-l Mulk and Malhar Rao invest Dehli, and Najibu-d daula is expelled—The Emperor proceeds to the eastern part of the country—Account of Kasim 'Ali Khan, Governor of Bengal—Nawab Shuja'u-d daula comes with the view of expelling Ahmad Khan Bangash—Death of Nawab Sa'du-llah Khan—Dundi Khan goes to Nawab Shuja'u-d daula to settle the dispute which was raised by Ahmad Khan Bangash—'Alamgir Badshah slain by the hands of Balabash Khan—Suraj Mal Jat killed—Jawahir Singh Jat besieges Najibu-d daula in Dehli—Government of Ratan Singh Jat, Kehri Singh and others—Flight of Nawab Shuja'u-d daula—His arrival at Katehr—Battle of Kora—The Nawab's interview with the English—Death of Nawab 'Abdu-llah Khan—Arrival of Ram Chandar, Ganesh, Madhuji Sindiya and others—Death of Ahmad Khan Bangash—Death of Dundi Khan—Death of Najibu-d daula, and authority acquired by Muhammad Zabita

Khan—March from Allahabad to Dehli, and defeat of Muhammad Zabita Khan—Account of Sarikar Gangapur—Death of Sardar Khan Bakhshi, and the exploits of his sons—Ahmad Khan and his son take possession of his dominions and wealth—Engagement between 'Inayat Khan and Hafizu-l Mulk—Release of the dependents of Zabita Khan—The Dakhin chiefs come to Ram Ghat—Dispute between Hafiz Rahmat Khan and Ahmad Khan, son of the deceased Bakhshi—Death of Fath Khan Khan-saman—Quarrels between his sons—Governor-General Lord (Warren) Hastings' arrival at Benares, and his interview with Nawab Shuj'au-d daula—Nawab Shuja'-d daula suggests the invasion of Katehr, and Hafizu-l Mulk is slain—Account of Muhammad Yar Khan after his death—Muhibu-llah Khan and Fathu-llah Khan—Account of the Begam of Nawab Sa'du-llah Khan—Interview between Mathu-llah Khan and Nawab Shuja'u-d daula—Nawab Shuja'u-d daula comes to Anwala—Interview between him and Nawab Muhammad Yar Khan—Interview of Muhibu-llah Khan with Najaf Khan and Ilich Khan—Nawab Shuja reaches Bisauli and encamps there—Muhammad Bashir comes to confiscate Anwala—Account of Yusuf Khan of Kandahar—Anwala confiscated and its inhabitants ruined—Nawab Shuja'u-d daula falls sick at Bisauli after the conquest—Discussion between Nawab Shuja'u-d daula and the General of the British army regarding their march from Laldong—Proposal of the former—The General's reply—Proposals and replies of Shuja'u-d daula—Shuja'u-d daula's letter to the Council of India—General Champion's letter to the same—Answer of the Council—Forty lacs of rupees sent to the members of the Council at Calcutta—Measures taken by the Nawab to protect the newly-conquered territory—Nawab Muhammad Yar Khan leaves Shuja'u-d daula—Expenses of the author's master—Death of Shuja'u-d daula—Government of Nawab Asafu'd daula, and resignation of Muhammad Ilich Khan—Ruin of Muhammad Bashir Khan—Advancement of Mulla Ahmad

2.

Khan, Himmat Bahadur and others—Death of Muhammad Mustakim Khan—Confiscation of the property of Nawab Sa'du-llah Khan's Begam at Faizabad—Liberty of prisoners obtained at the cost of three *lacs* of rupees—Ahmad Khan crosses the Ganges—Shahamat Khan, son of Bakhshi—Sa'adat Khan, son of ditto—Kallu Khan, son of ditto—Abu-l Kasim slain—Mukhtaru-d daula and Basant Khan killed—Mirza Sa'adat 'Ali proceeds to Agra—Arrival of Muhammad Ilich Khan from Agra.

HADIKATU-L AKALIM
OF
MURTAZA HUSAIN.

This is an admirable compilation, the celebrity of which is by no means in proportion to its merits. It is written on the model of the *Haft-Iklim*, but is far superior to the work of Ahmad Razi and all others I have seen, both in accuracy and research. Besides the geographical details of the work, there are various minor histories of the events succeeding the decline of the Mughal monarchy, and of the Mahrattas, Rohillas, and the Nawabs of Oudh, etc., which convey much information, derived not only from extensive reading, but close personal observation.

The author, Murtaza Husain, known as Shaikh Illah Yar 'Usmani of Bilgram, says of himself, that from 1142 to 1187 A.H. (1729 to 1773), *i.e.* from the times of Muhammad Shah to the middle of the reign of Shah 'Alam II, he had the honour of being employed under the following nobles of India: 1. Saiyid Sarbuland Khan Tuni; 2. Saiyid Sa'adat Khan Naishapuri; 3. Muhammad Kasim Khan; 4. 'Ali Kuli Khan 'Abbasi *shashangushti* or six-fingered; 5. Ahmad Khan; 6. Muhammad Khan Bangash of Farrukhabad, besides several others. On this account the opportunity was afforded him of being an actor in the scenes in which they were engaged. He was subsequently introduced, in A.H. 1190 (1776

A.D.), when he was in his forty-seventh year, by his friend Rajab 'Ali, to Captain Jonathan Scott, Persian Secretary to Warren Hastings, who immediately appointed him one of his *munshis*, "than which, in the opinion of English gentlemen, there is no higher office; and receiving encouragement from his employer's intelligence and love of learning, he was induced to undertake this work."

The *Hadikatu-l Akalim* contains a description of the Terrestrial Globe, its inhabited quarter, and the seven grand divisions of the later. A short account of the wonders and curiosities of every country, a brief account of the Prophets, great kings, philosophers, and celebrated and great men of many countries.

"Quotations," says the author, "from every existing work have been sometimes copied verbatim into this work, and sometimes, when the style of the original was too figurative, alterations have been made in the extracts, my object being that my readers might acquire some knowledge both of the ancient and modern style of the Persian language, and by observing its changes should be led to reflect that every sublunary thing is subject to change." The reason is somewhat curious, especially as that moral might be much more easily learnt from the political vicissitudes he undertakes to record.

The author moreover confesses that he has an eye to his own interest in this compilation. "If the work shall ever be persued by the intelligent and learned English, it is expected that, taking into their consideration the troubles and old age of the author, they will always do him the favour of maintaining their kind regards towards him and his descendants, especially as this was the first Persian work compiled under their auspices, which gave a history of the establishment of the British Empire." This supplication has been granted, and his son has been raised to high office under the British Government. He concludes by saying that this work was composed when he was in his sixtieth year, and was submitted for the inspection of Captain Scott and Colonel Polier before being engrossed.

It is probable that this work is amongst those used by Capt. Scott in his account of Aurangzeb's successors; but as in the two copies of his history which I have examined, the promised list of MS. authorities is not given, there is no knowing what were the materials which he used as the chief sources of his information.

SIZE—Large 8vo., 888 pages of 25 lines each.

EXTRACT

The British, after the rainy season, in the year 1178 A.H. (1764 A.D.), marched upon Baksar, and in a pitched battle defeated Shuja'u-d daula, who retreated to Lucknow. The conquerors advanced upon Allahabad, and laid siege to its strong fort, which surrendered after a short resistance; whereupon the Nawab was obliged to abandon all his dominions. The British had now under their entire control the conquered provinces; but they did not kill or plunder their subjects; nor did the rent-free holders and pensioners find any cause to complain. Shuja'u-d daula courted the alliance and support of Ahmad Khan Bangash, ruler of Farrukhabad, Hafiz Rahmat Khan, and Dundi Khan, chiefs of Rohilla, Bareilly, and Anwala, which they all declined. Then he repaired to Kalpi, but he was driven thence by the British.

At this time the Emperor of Dehli made an alliance with the British, and the district of Allahabad was assigned to him for his residence. He agreed to grant to the Company possession of the Bengal province, in return for which he was to receive annually twenty-five *lacs* of rupees. Moreover, seventy-five *lacs* were given to him as a present. After some years Muniru-d daula, revising the treaty, increased the payment to twenty-seven *lacs* of rupees; but when the Emperor returned to Dehli, the stipulated payments were withheld. Shuja'u-d daula, making peace with the English, was restored to his dominions of Oudh, where he soon gathered great strength. In a few years Ahmad Khan Bangash, Dundi Khan, and other famous Rohilla chiefs, departed this life, and of all the Rohilla chiefs there remained not one to raise the standard of sovereignty and Islam, except Hafiz Rahmat Khan, from Shah-Jahanpur, Bareilly, and Pilibhit, to Sambhal. Shuja'u-d daula, with the aid of the English, invaded the territories of Hafiz Rahmat, who was killed in battle; but the victory was entirely owing to British valour. The Rohilla country then came into the power of Shuja'u-d daula, and great distress fell upon it, for it was given up to his unrestrained desires. At length the Nawab's excessive indulgence brought on him a severe disease. By the British directions he made a treaty with Faizu-llah Khan, son of 'Ali Muhammad Khan Rohilla, who obtained under it his hereditary estates of Rampur. Shuja'u-d daula, still labouring under his tormenting disease, removed from Laldong to Oudh, and there died. His son, Mirza Mani, succeeded him, with the title of *Asafu-d daula*.

JAM-I JAHAN-NUMA
OF
KUDRATU-LLAH

The "World-reflecting Mirror" was written by Shaikh Kudratu-llah Sadiki, an inhabitant of Mavi, near the town of Kabar in Rohilkhand. He quotes several authorities of the ordinary stamp, as well as all those mentioned in the *Khulasatu-t Tawarikh*, which he would evidently wish the incautious reader to believe were consulted by him also in original.

There is nothing novel in the work, but the biographies at the end are useful. It was commenced in the year 1191 A.H. (1777 A.D.), and bears the same date at the end; but this is evidently a mistake, for, at the close of the Dehli history, events are brought down to the year 1193 A.H. (1779 A.D.), "when twenty years had elapsed of the reign of Shah 'Alam, and in every corner of the kingdom people aspired to exercise independence. Allahabad, Oudh, Etawah, Shukohabad, and the whole country of the Afghans (Rohillas) are in the possession of the Nawab Wazir Asafu-d daula, and the whole country of Bengal has been subjected by the strong arm of the Firingis. The country of the Jats is under Najaf Khan, and the Dakhin is partly under Nizam 'Ali Khan, partly under the Mahrattas, and partly under Haidar Naik and Muhammad 'Ali Khan Siraju-d daula of Gopamau. The Sikhs hold the whole *suba* of the Panjab, and Lahore, and Multan; and Jainagar and other places are held by Zabita Khan. In this manner other *zamindars* have established themselves here and there. All the world is waiting in anxious expectation of the appearance of Imam Mahdi, who is to come in the latter days. Shah 'Alam sits in the palace of Dehli, and has no thought beyond the gratification of his own pleasure, while his people are deeply sorrowful and grievously oppressed even unto death." It is to be regretted that these desponding anticipations are not occasionally reverted to by the present fortunate generation.

The author gives us some information respecting himself at the close of his work. He tells us that his progenitors arrived in India as early as the time of Pirthi Raj, and that he had a large body of foreign cavalry under his command at Sonpat. Some of his ancestors are buried in Sonpat and Ajmir, where they died waging holy wars. In course of time they moved into Rohilkhand, and Raja Taj Khan, of the Katehrzai clan, bestowed Mavi and twelve other villages in Kabar upon the family. There they have continued to reside, and amongst them have appeared several prodigies of excellence and learning. In the course of their genealogy, he states many anachronisms and other improbabilities, which throw doubt upon the correctness of the family tree.

CONTENTS

Preface, p. 1—Introduction, Creation and Pre-Adamite Eras, p. 8—Chapter I. Adam and the Prophets, p. 27—II. Philosophers, p. 144—III. Kings of Persia, in four Sections (*makalas*), p. 150—IV. Kings of Arabia before Islam, p. 197—V. The Prophet Muhammad, in five Sections, p. 206—VI. The 'Ummayide Khalifs, p. 362—VII. The 'Abbaside Khalifs, p. 402—VIII. to XX. The Samanis, Ghaznivides, Ghorians, and other Dynasties, p. 421—XXI. Khundkars of Rum, p. 491—XXII. Kaissaras of Rum, p. 494—XXIII. The Khans of the Turks, in three Sections, p. 511—XXIV. Changiz Khan and his sons, in four Sections, p. 514—XXV. Branches of the Mughals, p. 540—XXVI. Timur and his sons, p. 546—XXVII. The Uzbaks, p. 563—XXVIII. The Safavis, p. 565—XXIX. The seven Climates and the Subas of Hindustan, in two Sections, p. 570—XXX. The Rajas of Hindustan, in fifteen Sections, p. 592—XXXI. The Sultans of Hindustan from Muhammad Sam to the present time, in five Sections, p. 630—XXXII. to XXXIX. Sultans of the Dakhin, Gujarat, Thatta, Bengal, Jaunpur, Malwa, Kashmir, and Multan, p. 864—Conclusion, Biographies of learned Doctors, Devotees and Saints, and a brief account of the Author, p. 925.

The only copy which I know of this work is a very clean and correct one, in the library of Sa'idu-d din Ahmad Khan, a gentleman of Muradabad.

SIZE—4to., 1378 pages of 21 lines each.

MA-ASIRU-L UMARA
OF
SHAH NAWAZ KHAN SAMSAMU-D DAULA

[This work may be called the Peerage of the Mughal Empire.] It consists of a Biographical Dictionary of the illustrious men who have flourished in Hindustan and the Dakhin under the house of Timur from Akbar to 1155 A.H.

["Amir Kamalu-d din, the fifth ancestor of Shah Nawaz Khan, came from Khwaf to Hindustan in the reign of Akbar, whose service he entered; and his descendants held in succession some of the highest offices of State under the succeeding Emperors. Shah Nawaz Khan, whose original name was 'Abdu-r Razzak al Husaini, was born at Lahore in 1111 A.H. (1699 A.D.). Early in life he went to Aurangabad, where most of his relatives resided, and he was not long afterwards appointed *Diwan* of Birar. Having incurred the displeasure of Nizamu-l Mulk Asaf Jah, by favouring the revolt of his son Nasir Jang, he was disgraced, and went into retirement. It was during this period that he composed the *Ma-asiru-l Umara*. After he had passed five years in seclusion, Asaf Jah, in 1160 A.H. (1747 A.D.), shortly before his death, took him again into favour, and reinstated him in the *Diwani* of Birar. Shah Nawaz Khan enjoyed the highest honours under Nasir Jang, the son and successor of Asaf Jah, and subsequently became the chief minister of Salabat Jang, the *Subadar* of the Dakhin, and played a conspicious part in the affairs of that portion of India, and the struggles for supremacy between the English and French. He was assassinated in 1171 A.H. (1757 A.D.). Ghulam 'Ali implicates Bussy in his murder, but the charge appears to be without foundation, the native historian being no doubt misled by his prejudices.']

The work was commenced by Shah Nawaz Khan Samsamu-d daula, but he left it unfinished, and in the turbulent scenes which succeeded his death, his house was plundered, and his manuscript scattered in various directions. It was considered as lost, till Mir Ghulam 'Ali, surnamed Azad, the author of two biographical works, the *Saru-i Azad* and *Khazana-i Amira*,[1] and a

[1] *Though professedly a Biography of Persian Poets, the Khazana-i Amira contains a very full account of the transactions of a great portion of the last century, the*

friend of Shah Nawaz Khan, collected the greater portion of the missing leaves, and restored the work to its entire form with a few additions, amongst which was the life of the author,[2] and a preface, which gives an account of the work.

["Ghulam 'Ali was a poet and a biographer of poets. He was born in 1116 A.H. (1704 A.D.), but the date of his death is not known. He was at one time attached to Samsamu-d daula in the capacity of amanuensis. He travelled into various parts of India, and visited Mecca and Medina, and, according to the *Khulasatu-l Afkar*, "after his journeys and pilgrimage he was much honoured, during his residence at Aurangabad, by the *Subadars*, and associated in friendly intimacy with the sons of Nizamu-l Mulk Asaf Jah; yet with these temptations he never engaged in the affairs of the world.'

"The biographies comprised in the first edition of the work extend to Ghulam 'Ali's own time, and are 261 in number, including the life of the author by the editor.'"]

At a subsequent period the son of Samsamu-d daula, named 'Abdu-l Hai Khan, completed the work in its present form, giving insertion to his father's original Introduction, and to the Introduction of Mir Ghulam 'Ali. So the work as it at present stands contains ["The Preface by the Editor.—The Original Preface of Shah Nawaz Khan.—The Preface by Ghulam 'Ali—The Life of Shah Nawaz Khan by Ghulam 'Ali—An Index to the Biographies.—The Biographies arranged in alphabetical order.—Conclusion, containing a short life of the Editor, 'Abdu-l Hai Khan."]

author taking every opportunity of interweaving historical matter in his narrative. The passages relative to the Nawabs of Oudh occupy about one-fifth of the entire work.

[2]*Translated by H. H. Wilson, in the Oriental Quarterly Magazine, vol. iv.*

["The biographies in the second edition are 731 in number, giving an increase of 569 lives not contained in the former edition. They are very ably written, and are full of important historical detail; and as they include the lives of all the most eminent men who flourished in the time of the Mughal Emperors of the House of Timur down to 1194 A.H. (1780 A.D.), the *Ma-asiru-l umara* must always hold its place as one of the most valuable books of reference for the student of Indian History. 'Abdu-l Hai enumerates no less than thirty histories and biographical treatises from which he has drawn the materials for his portion of the work."]

Colonel Stewart has curiously confused the names of the authors of the *Ma-asiru-l umara*. He has completely reversed the relations of father and son, observing, "This book was compiled by 'Abdu-l Hai bin 'Abdu-r Razzak Shah Nawaz Khan, and finished by his son Samsamu-d daula A.D. 1779."[3] He has repeated the error in the list of authorities prefixed to his History of Bengal. He appears to have been misled by the latter nobleman's different appellations; his name being 'Abdu-r Razzak, and his titles successively Shah Nawaz Khan and Samsamu-d daula.

["'Abdu-l Hai Khan was born in 1142 A.H. (1729 A.D.), and in 1162 A.H. (1748 A.D.) was elevated to the rank of Khan by Nizam Nasir Jang, who also bestowed upon him the *Diwani* of Birar. In the time of Salabat Jang he became commandant of Daulatabad. On his father's murder in 1171 A.H. (1757 A.D.), he was imprisoned in the fortress of Golkonda, but he was subsequently released in 1173 A.H. (1759 A.D.) by Nizamu-d daula Asaf Jah II., who treated him with great distinction, and reinstated him in his paternal title as Samsamu-l Mulk. He died in 1196 A.H. (1781 A.D.). 'Abdu-l Hai's title varies in a rather perplexing way. It was at first Shamsu-d daula Dilawar Jang. When he was released from prison,

---

[3]*Cat. of Tippoo's Library, p.* 19.

he received his father's title, and became Samsamu-d-daula Samsam Jang. In his Appendix to the *Ma-asiru-l umara* he calls himself Samsamu-l Mulk, and gives his poetical name as *Sarim*. Bland refers to a work in which he is called Samsamu-l Mulk Dilawar Jang."⁴]

Size—Fol. 17 in. by 11¼, 421 pages, 25 lines in a page.

EXTRACTS

Mahabat Khan Khan-khanan Sipah-salar

Zamana Beg was son of Ghuyur Beg Kabuli, and belonged to the Saiyids of the pure Razwiya stock. Khan-zaman, son of Mahabat Khan, in a history which he wrote, traces the descent of his ancestors from the Prophet Moses. They were all men of position and wealth. Ghuyur Beg came from Shiraz to Kabul, and settled among one of the tribes of that neighbourhood. He was enrolled among the military followers of Mirza Muhammad Hakim, and on the death of the Mirza he obtained employment in the service of the Emperor Akbar, when he distinguished himself greatly in the campaign against Chitor. Zamana Beg in his youth was entered among the *ahadis* of Prince Salim (Jahangir), and, having rendered some acceptable services, he, in a short time, received a suitable *mansab*, and was made *Bakhshi* of the *shagird-peshas*. When Raja Uchaina made a treaty and agreement with Mu'azzam Khan Fathpuri at Allahabad, and came to wait upon the Prince, the city and its environs swarmed with his numerous followers. Whenever he went out, all men, high and low, gazed with wondering eyes at his followers. This annoyed the Prince, who said one night in private, "Why should I be troubled with this man?" Zamana Beg said that if permission were given, he would that very night settle his business. Having received directions, he went alone with a servant at midnight to the dwelling of the Raja, who was drunk

⁴*A large portion of this article has been taken from Morley's Catalogue.*

and fast asleep. He left his servant at the door, and telling the Raja's servants to wait outside, because he had a royal message to deliver, he went into the tent, cut off the Raja's head, wrapped it in a shawl, and came out. Telling the servants that no one must go in, because he had an answer to bring, he took the head and threw it down before the Prince. Orders were immediately given for plundering the Raja's followers. When these discovered what had happened, they dispersed, and all the Raja's treasure and animals were confiscated to the State. Zamana Beg received the title of Mahabat Khan, and at the beginning of the reign of Jahangir he was raised to *mansab* of 3,000, and sent in command of an army against the Rana.[5] . . .

Mu'tamad Khan

Mu'tamad Khan Muhammad Sharif was a native of Persia, of obscure station. On his coming to India his good fortune caused his introduction to Jannat Makani (Jahangir). In the third year of the reign he was honoured with the title of Mu'tamad Khan. He was *Bakhshi* of the *Ahadis* for a long time. In the ninth year died Sulaiman Beg Fidai Khan, who was *Bakhshi* of the army of Prince Shah Jahan in the campaign against the Rana. Mu'tamad Khan was then appointed to the office. In the eleventh year, when the Prince was deputed to make arrangements in the Dakhin, the office of *Bakhshi* was again entrusted to him. . . . Although he had a reputation for his knowledge of history, yet it appears from his work *Ikbalnama Jahangiri*, which is written in an easy flowing style, that he had very little skill in historical writing, as, notwithstanding his holding the office of *Ahad-navisi*, he has not only left out many trifling matters, but has even narrated imperfectly important facts.

[*The subsequent career of this nobleman occupies a leading place in the history of the reigns of Jahangir and Shah Jahan.*]

TAZKIRATU-L UMARA
OF
KEWAL RAM

This is a Biographical account of the nobles of Hindustan, from the time of Akbar to Bahadur Shah, by Kewal Ram, son of Raghunath Das Agarwala, inhabitant of Kasma in Bulandshahr, written in the year 1194 A.H. (1780 A.D.). It gives an account of all dignitaries above the *mansab* of two hundred, and of the Hindu Rajas who distinguished themselves during that period. It contains very little more than the patents of nobility, privileges and insignia bestowed upon each person, and the occasion of his promotion. It is altogether a very meagre compilation compared with the *Ma-asiru-l Umara*.

SIZE—8vo., 701 pages of 16 lines each.

SAWANIH-I AKBARI
OF
AMIR HAIDAR HUSAINI

[This is a modern history of the Emperor Akbar, written by Amir Haidar Husaini Wasiti of Bilgram, whose ancestors came from Wasit in Arabia. The work was compiled at the instance of "Mufakhkharu-d daula Bahadur Shaukat-i Jang William Kirkpatrick," and so must have been written towards the close of the last century. It bears no date, and unfortunately extends only to the end of the twenty-fourth year of the reign. The author states that he derived his materials from the *Akbar-nama* of Abu-l Fazl, the *Muntakhab* of Badayuni, the *Tabakat* of Nizamu-d din Ahmad, Firishta, the *Akbar-nama* of Illahdad Faizi Sihrindi, the *Ma-asiru-l umara* and other works. He adds that he used the four parts of the *Insha-e Abu-l Fazl*, and especially mentions the fourth part, expressing his surprise that it has been so little refered to by historians. The *Insha* is a well known work, and has often been printed, but in three parts only; so, Blochmann says, "it looks as if Amir Haidar's copy of the fourth part was unique." But a reference made by Sir H. Elliot in Vol. V. of this work, (original ed.) shows that he had access to this rare portion of the work. The *Akbar-nama* of Abu-l Fazl is the authority mainly relied upon, and the author says he "has omitted those superfluities of language which Abu-l Fazl employed for rhetorical purposes."

"This work," adds Blochmann, "is perhaps the only critical historical work written by an Indian," and he particularly recommends it to the notice of European historians.*

SIZE—Large 8vo., 843 pages of 15 lines each.]

SIYARU-L MUTA-AKHKHIRIN
OF
GHULAM HUSAIN KHAN.

[The first part of this work gives a general description of Hindustan, of its provinces, cities, products and people. It also gives summary of the ancient history as derived from the Sanskrit works translated by Faizi and others. It then notices the rise of the Muhammadan power, and adds a succinct history of the reigns of the various sovereign down to the death of Aurangzeb. This constitutes the first volume of the work, and its contents are generally identical with those of the *Khulasatu-t Tawarikh*. The author has been severely condemned by Col. Lees[1] for glaring plagiarism in having stated that he derived his matter from the work of an old *munshi*, without ever mentioning the name of the author of the *Khulasatu-t Tawarikh*. It has been shown by Sir H. M. Elliot, that the *Khulasatu-t Tawarikh* itself is a gross piracy of an anonymous work called *Mukhta-*

[*Ain-i Akbari, vol. i. pp. xxxi. and 316.]
[1][*Journal of Royal Asiatic Society*, N.S. vol. iii.]

siru-t Tawarikh, and it may have been this very work that Ghulam Husain used and referred to as the production of "some old *munshi*."]

[It is the second volume of the work that has become famous, and to which the title *Siyaru-l Muta-akhkhirin*,[2] "Review of Modern Times," is particularly applicable.] This consists of a general history of India from 1700 to 1786 A.D. It contains the reigns of the last seven Emperors of Hindustan, an account of the progress of the English in Bengal up to 1781 A.D., and a critical examination of their government and policy in Bengal. The author treats these important subjects with a freedom and spirit, and with a force, clearness and simplicity of style very unusual in an Asiatic writer, and which justly entitles him to pre-eminence among Muhammadan historians. ["It is written," says General Briggs, "in the style of private memoirs, the most useful and engaging shape which history can assume; nor, excepting in the peculiarities which belong to the Muhammadan character and creed, do we perceive throughout its pages any inferiority to the historical memoirs of Europe. The Duc de Sully, Lord Clarendon or Bishop Burnet need not have been ashamed to be the authors of such a production."]

The testimony which Ghulam Husain bears to the merits of the English is on the whole creditable to them. Dr. Tennant observes that "of injustice and corruption, as judges, the author entirely acquits our countrymen; and of cruelty and oppression, as rulers, he brings not the slightest imputation. From his intimate acquaintance with this subject, and his bias, if he felt any, being

[2][*Writers dsiagree as to the exact reading and meaning of the title. It may be Sairu-l Muta-akhkhirin, "Review of Modern Times," which seems to be favoured by the French translator and the Calcutta editor,—or Siyaru-l Muta-akhkhirin, "Manners of the Moderns," as rendered by Briggs, and followed by Sir H. M. Elliot.*]

wholly against us, we may applaud our early adventurers for having obtained this honourable testimony to their character. From want of knowledge in the language, he does accuse them of sometimes having suffered themselves to be imposed on by their *banians* and *sarkars;* nor does he conceal that injustice was sometimes committed through their interference. Persian writings and books are not committed to the press and disseminated by publication as in Europe. This author's MSS., for many years, were handed about privately among the Indians. He could, therefore, have no fear of giving offence to the English by what he brought forward. This is indeed apparent from many strictures he has written abundantly severe; nor does there seem any intention to please by flattery in a work that was never submitted to the perusal of the English. The praises of General Goddard, and of many other individuals, to be found in the *Siyaru-l Muta-akhkhirin*, are no exception to this remark, since they are evidently the effusions of sincerity and gratitude, and some of them, as that of Fullarton, were written long after parties concerned had left the country. Without having any knowledge of civil liberty in the abstract, this author possessed the fullest enjoyment of it, and from this circumstance his testimony has become of great importance."[3]

The *Siyaru-l Muta-akhkhirin*, or "Manners of the Moderns," was completed in the year 1783 by Saiyid Ghulam 'Ali Khan Tabataba, a relation of Nawab 'Aliwardi Khan. His father, Hidayat 'Ali Khan, held the Government of Bihar in the *subadarship* of Mahabat Jang, as the *naib*, or deputy, of his nephew and son-in-law Haibat Jang. He was afterwards *Faujdar*, or military governor, of Sonpat and Panipat, in the reign of Muhammad Shah. On the flight of Shah 'Alam from Dehli to avoid the persecution of Ghaziu-d din Khan, he accompanied him as his *Mir-bakhshi* or chief paymaster;

[3] *Tennant's Indian Recreations, vol. i. p. 286.*

having obtained for his eldest son Ghulam Husain, the post of *Mirmunshi* or principal secretary; and for his second son Fakhru-d daula, that of *Diwan-i tan* or overseer of the household. The necessities of the Prince at length compelled Hidayat 'Ali to relinquish his station, and he retired to his *jagir* in Bihar, where he died soon after the deposition of Kasim 'Ali Khan.

His son, Ghulam Haidar, afterwards acted as representative of Kasim 'Ali Khan in Calcutta, till his suspected attachment to the English occasioned his removal. He was then engaged in various services under our own Government, and received many marks of favour from General Goddard, whom he attended on several enterprises. In a short Preface he says, "No one apparently having stood forth to write an account of the nobles of Hind since the death of Aurangzeb, I will briefly record what I know on the subject, or have heard from trustworthy and esteemed narrators, to the end that if hereafter any intelligent historian should be inclined to write the events of former times, the thread of successive occurrences might not be entirely broken. Relying, therefore, on the Divine aid, I proceed to the execution of my task, and will put down in clear language, free from abstruseness, whatsoever I have heard related by persons considered worthy of credit. If any mistakes occur, my apology is evident: those who have furnished this information must be answerable."

Some further particulars of the author may be found in volumes ii. and iii. of the *Asiatic Annual Register*, in which Extracts are given from his autobiography, which is said to have been prefixed to his History, but it does not appear there in the printed edition by 'Abdu-l Majid.

This work was translated into English by Mustafa, a French renegade, and published at Calcutta in 1789 in three quarto volumes. The history of the translator is not very well known, but it appears from his Preface that he was in English employ, that he was a Muham-

3.

madan, and that he was plundered during a pilgrimage to Mecca. He was a French, Italian, Turkish, and apparently a classical scholar, also a perfect master of Persian and Hindustani. But although he prided himself upon his knowledge of English, he was not throughly versed in our tongue, and it is to be regretted that his translation was made into a language of which he was not a master, for his version is full of Gallicisms, although he says that he "could not write in any other language so fluently." A large portion of the impression of his work was lost on its way to England, [and it has long been a rare book, only to be found here and there in public libraries.]

General Briggs undertook to bring out a new translation, [but he published only one volume, containing about one-sixth of the whole work, and this was more an amended version of the original translator's English than a revision of his translation.] A portion of the work relating to the transactions in Bengal has been translated in the second volume of Scott's *History of the Deccan*.

The *Siyaru-l Muta-akhkhirin* has been printed more than once at Calcutta. An excellent edition of the first volume was brought out there in 1836 by Hakim 'Abdu-l Majid, in a quarto volume of 534 pages.

The work is well known to English readers from the many quotations and abstracts which Mill has made from it in his *History of India;* [and Ghulam Husain is "the Musulman historian of those times" whom Macaulay has quoted and spoken of with approval.[4] In fact, the native side of the history of Ghulam Husain's days, as it appears in the works of English writers, rests almost entirely upon his authority. The limits of the present volume will not allow of such lengthy extracts as the merits of the work require, and it seems preferable to bring forward the views and statements of other writers,

Essay on Clive.

most of whom are entirely unknown to the European reader. For these reasons no Extracts from the work are here given; but it is greatly to be desired that a complete translation of this history should be accessible to the students of Indian history.]

MULAKHKHASU-T TAWARIKH
OF
FARZAND 'ALI HUSAIN

This is an abridgment of the *Siyaru-l Muta-akhkhirin* by Farzand 'Ali of Monghir, who says respecting himself:

"Being highly desirous to learn the history of the great kings of former times, I employed myself in the study of the *Siyaru-l Muta-akhkhirin*, the unrivalled composition of Ghulam 'Ali Khan. As this book has many beauties and advantages, which are rarely found in any other work on history, it has ever been dear to my heart; but its extreme prolixity not only demands a long time for its perusal, but exhausts the patience of readers; so at the request of some of my friends, I made an abstract of the work, and denominated it *Mulakhkhasu-t Tawarikh*."

This work is divided into three parts. Part I. Brief account of the Kings of India, from the reign of Timur to the twenty-second year of Muhammad Shah, 1738 A.D. Part II. A full account of the transactions in Bengal, 'Azimabad, and Orissa, to the commencement of the English rule in 1781 A.D. Part III. Transactions from the twenty-second year of Muhammad Shah up to the twenty-third year of Shah 'Alam's reign, 1781 A.D.

It has been printed in a quarto volume, containing 511 pages of 19 lines each.

There is another abridgment of the *Siyaru-l Muta-akhkhirin* by Maulavi 'Abdu-l Karim, Head Master of the Persian Office. It was printed in Calcutta in one volume quarto in 1827, under the name of *Zubdatu-t Tawarikh*.

TARIKH-I MAMALIK-I HIND
OF
GHULAM BASIT

This is a compilation by Ghulam Basit, undertaken at the suggestion of an English officer. The title is the one borne by the copy at Bombay which I have had the opportunity of consulting. [But there is a work bearing the title of *Tarikh-i Basit*, which is probably the same as this.]

The author tells us of himself, that he had no excellence of person or mind, and was long living on the income of a few acres of land which had descended to him from his ancestors, when, to his misfortune, his tenure, along with the other rent-free tenures in the province of Oudh, was resumed, and he was consequently reduced to the greatest distress and embarrassment. The author in this emergency wished that, like his ancestors, who for about three hundred years had been in the service of the Emperors of Hindustan, he also might enter the service of the same family. But although, he observes, there were thousands and hundreds of thousands of people as insignificant as himself, who, notwithstanding the decline of the empire, subsisted upon the bounty of that house, he through his bad luck was disappointed in that expectation, and was obliged to seek employment under the English, who were noted for their generosity and courage. He assumed the name of a *munshi* in order to secure his daily bread, and through the grace of God and the kindness of his masters, he at last obtained a sufficient provision for himself and children, and prayed God for the welfare of the English who had supported him.

In the year 1196 A.H. (1782 A.D.) he went to Calcutta, in company with I'tikadu-d daula Nasiru-l Mulk General Charles Burt, who one day requested him to write a brief account of the Rulers of Hindustan, whether Musulman or Hindu, on the authority both of books and of oral testimony. As he considered gratitude paramount to all other obligations, he abstracted preceding authors, and noted down all that he had heard from his father Shaikh Saifu-llah of Bijnor, who had been during his whole life in the royal service, and had attained the great age of one hundred and five years. Although he abridged the accounts derived from other historians, he did so without the omission of any material points; and on the conclusion of his work, delivered one copy to his patron, and retained one for himself.

He does not state from what works he compiled his history; but in the course of it he mentions incidentally, amongst others, the *Mahabharat, Matla'u-l Anwar, Tarikh-i Bahadur-shahi, Tarikh-i Yamini*, the histories of Haji Muhammad Kandahari and Nizamu-d din Ahmad. As these are all mentioned by Firishta, it is probable he only quotes them at second-hand.

He appears to have taken a very short time about the compilation, for he brings it down to the 10th of Ramazan of the same year in which he commenced it, namely, 1196 A.H. (1782 A.D.), the twenty-fourth year of Shah 'Alam's reign, upon whose head he invokes a blessing.

The work is not divided into regular Books and Chapters. He begins with the Creation, proceeds from the Patriarchs, Hindu Demigods and Rajas to the Ghaznivides and Sultans of Dehli down to the reigning monarch. Before treating of the Timurian Sovereigns, he introduces an account of the Rulers of Sind, Multan, Kashmir, Bengal, Jaunpur, the Bahmanis, the Kings of Bijapur, Ahmadnagar, Birar, Gujarat, Malwa, Khandesh and Malabar.

I know of only two copies of this history. One belonged to the late Mulla Firoz of Bombay, and another I saw at Kanauj with the title *Zubdatu-t Tawarikh*.

[The Extract was translated by a *munshi*, and revised by Sir H. M. Elliot.]

SIZE—8vo., 612 pages of 17 lines each.

EXTRACTS

In 1020 A.H. (1611 A.D.), the Emperor Nuru-d din Jahangir made over the fort of Surat, in the province of Gujarat, to the English, against whom the Firingis of Portugal bear a most deadly enmity, and both are thirsty of each other's blood. This was the place where the English made their first settlement in India. For instance, they consider Jesus Christ (may the peace of God rest on him!) a servant of God and His prophet, but do not admit that he was the Son of God. They are in no wise obedient to the King of Portugal, but have their own king. At present, A.H. 1196 (1782 A.D.), these people have sway over most parts of Hindustan.

The people of Malibar are for the most part infidels, and their chief is called Ghaiar (Ghamyar?). Their marriage ceremony consists in tying some writing round the neck of the bride, but this is not of much effect, for women are not restricted to one marriage. One woman may have several husbands, and she cohabits every night with one of them by turns. The carpenters, blacksmiths, dyers, in short, all except Brahmins, form connexions with each other in this fashion.

Originally the infidel Khokhars of the Panjab, before embracing Islam, observed a very curious custom. Among them also polyandry prevailed. When one husband went into the house of the woman, he left something at the door as a signal, so that, if another husband happened to come at the same time, he might upon seeing it return. Besides this, if a daughter was born, she was taken out of the house immediately, and it was proclaimed, "Will any person purchase this girl, or not?" If there appeared any purchaser, she was given to him; otherwise she was put to death.

It is also a custom among the Malibaris, that in case of there being several brothers, none except the eldest is allowed to marry, because in that case there would be many heirs, and disputes might arise. If any of the other brothers desires a woman, he must go to some common strumpet of the *bazar*, but he cannot marry. If the eldest brother die, the survivors are to keep mourning for him during a whole year; and so on in proportion for the other brothers. Amongst them women make their advances to the men.

The Malibaris are divided into three classes. If a person of the highest class cohabit with one of the lowest, he is not allowed to eat until he has bathed, and if he should so eat, he is sold by the governor to the people of the lowest class, and is made a slave; unless he manages to escape to some place where he is not recognized. In the same manner, a person of the lowest class cannot cook for one of the highest; and if the latter eats food from the hands of the former, he is degraded from his class.

CHAHAR GULZAR SHUJA'I
OF
HARI CHARAN DAS

THE author of this work is Hari Charan Das, son of Udai Rai, son of Mukund Rai, son of Sagar Mal, late *chaudhari* and *kanungo* of the *pargana* of Mirat, in the province of Dehli. He tells us that he was in the employment of Nawab Kasim 'Ali Khan; and in the first year of the reign of 'Alamgir II., he accompained the Nawab and his daughter, Najbu-n Nisa Khanam, *alias* Bibi Khanam, wife of the late Nawab, Najamu-d daula Is'hak Khan, when they proceeded to Oudh, to have an interview with Nawab Mirza 'Ali Khan Iftikharu-d daula and Salar Jang Khan-khanan, the brothers of the deceased Nawab, and sons of Nawab Mu'tamadu-d daula Is'hak Khan.

Kasim 'Ali Khan, immediately after his arrival at Faizabad, departed this world, and the death of that noble man was a heavy blow to all his relations and friends. The complier, after this lamentable event, was, however, kindly retained in the service of the daughter of the deceased Nawab and his sons Shafik 'Ali Khan and Aka 'Ali Khan. Shafik 'Ali Khan, the elder brother, was much affected by the death of his father, and survived him only a few years. He was succeeded by his son, Hasain 'Ali Khan, who, having the same favourable regard which his father had towards the compiler, permitted him, through the recommendation of Naibu-n Nisa Begam, to continue to receive his allowance.

Although the family of the deceased Nawab was so kindly disposed towards him, yet, on account of some events which he promises to detail, a considerable change took place in his circumstances, and he was not so comfortably situated as before. Having no employment which could occupy his attention, and not wishing to waste his time in idleness, he devoted himself to the study of histories and biographical accounts of the ancient Kings. In this agreeable pursuit he was liberally assisted by Ibrahim 'Ali Khan, *alias* Mirza Khairati, son of Hikmat-ma'ab Khan, physician to the Emperor Ahmad Shah. This learned man was a near relation of the deceased Nawab Kasim 'Ali Khan, and had come with him to Faizabad. He was one of the greatest scholars of the time, and had a tolerable knowledge of mathematics and other sciences. He had collected a large number of historical and other works, and spent a great part of his time in their study. Being acquainted with the circumstances and duties of the compiler, he kindly lent him several works on history, such as *Firishta, Habibu-s Siyar, Mirat-i 'alam, Khulasatu-l Akhbarat,* and others. But not satisfied with the perusal of these books, the compiler also carefully went through the *Shak-nama, Rajavali, Ramayana, Mahabharat, Bhagavat,* Faizi's translation of the *Jog Bashist* from the Sanskrit into Persian, which he had in his own possession, besides other works which he borrowed from his friends.

Having by these means obtained an acquaintance with the history of ancient times, he wished to compile a work which might embrace an account of the Rajas, and Nobles of past ages, according to the information derived from the books above enumerated. He also designed to continue his work up to the 1199th year of the Hijra era (1785 A.D.), to produce a history of contemporary Kings and Amirs, and of those noblemen in whose employment he had been, noticing at the same time all the facts of historical importance which occurred under his own observation during his long life of eighty years. To this he also intended to add a sketch of his own and of his ancestor's lives, that he might leave a memorial to posterity.

From the time that the writer came to Oudh, some allowance for his maintenance was made by Nawab Shuja'u-d daula, through the recommendation of Babi Khanam and Shafik 'Ali Khan, and he continued to receive it for seventeen years, that is, up to 1184 A.H. (1770 A.D.), when it was stopped by Beni Bahadur, on account of some misunderstanding which arose between him and Babi Khanam. This involved the writer in great pecuniary distress, but after a few years, when Beni Bahadur became blind, and was deprived of his authority, an order was passed for restoring the payments which had been withheld. Although this was effected through the favour of Babi Khanam, in whose immediate employment he was, yet he considered it his duty to make some return for the obligations which he was under to Nawab Shuja'u-d daula; and "as that nobleman took great delight in gardens and orchards, and as every chapter of this work gives no less pleasure to the mind than a walk through the parterrs of a garden, the compiler thought it proper to dedicate it to him, and gave it therefore the title of *Chahar Gulzar Shuja'i*, "The Four Rose Gardens of Shuja'."

The work is nevertheless divided into five Books, fancifully styled *Chamans*, or "paterres," an apparent inconsistency derived from the fact that four is a favourite number, especially with respect to gardens, which, being generally square after the Oriental fashion, are divided into four even portions, by two transverse roads.

[The preceding account of the work was taken by Sir H. M. Elliot from the author's Preface. The writer is very communicative in other parts of his work as to his family and pecuniary matters, and he frequently enters into long details about them and his employments. He lived to the age of eighty, and had seen many of the events which he describes, so that his work is of value, though it is somewhat discursive. The Extracts all relate to modern times. They were translated for Sir H. M. Elliot by *munshis*, and have been corrected in his handwriting.]

CONTENTS

Book I. History of Brahma, Mahes, etc.—II. Account of the Satya Yuga—III. The Treta Yuga and the Avatars—IV. The Dwapara—V. The Kali Yuga; this book is divided into two parts.

Part I.—The Rajas of Dehli, now called Shah-Jahanabad, from the beginning of the Kali Yuga, or the reign of Raja Judhishtir, in whose time the great war took place, up to the first irruption of the Muhammadans, as taken from the *Rajavali* and Faizi's translation of the *Mahabharata* from Hindi into Persian.

Part II.—History of the Muhammadans, according to the most authentic works, and the author's own observation during a long life, from the establishment of their power in India to this the eightieth year of his age, and the 1198th of the Muhammadan era, corresponding with the twenty-fifth of Shah 'Alam's reign.

Part I.—Sec. i. Commences from Raja Judhishtir. Thirty Rajas of this line ruled during a period of 1799 years 5 months and 16 days. The following are their names :—ii. Raja Bisarwa and ... his successors, fourteen in number, reigned 500 years 2 months and 23 days.—iii. Raja Bir Bahu and ... his successors, sixteen in number, reigned 430 years 5 months—iv. Raja Dihandar and

... his successors, nine in number, reigned 359 years 11 months and 27 days.—v. Raja Sakot.—vi. Raja Bikramajit.—vii. Samundarpal; Jundpal, son of Samundarpal; Neipal, son of Jundpal; Despal, son of Neipal; Nar Singh Pal, son of Despal; Sabhpal, son of Nar Singh Pal; Lakhpal, son of Sabhpal; Gobindpal, son of Lakhpal; Sarbpal, son of Gobindpal; Balipal, son of Sarbpal; Mehrpal, son of Balipal; Harpal, son of Mehrpal; Bhimpal, son of Harpal; Madanpal, son of Bhimpal; Karmpal, son of Madanpal; Bikrampal, son of Karmpal. The reigns of these sixteen princes make up a period of 685 years 5 months and 20 days.—viii. Raja Tilok Chand; Bikram Chand, son of Tilok Chand; Kartik Chand, son of Bikram Chand; Ram Chand, son of Kartik Chand; Adhar Chand, son of Ram Chand; Kalyan Chand, son of Adhar Chand; Bhim Chand, son of Kalyan Chand; Girah Chand, son of Bhim Chand; Gobind Chand, son of Girah Chand; Rani Premvati, wife of Gobind Chand. These ten princes ruled during a period of 119 years 11 months and 9 days.—ix. Har Prem. Four Rajas of this family reigned during 49 years 11 months and 20 days. —Gobind Chand, son of Har Prem; Gopal Prem, son of Gobind Chand; Maha Patr, son of Gopal Prem.—x. Dahi Sen; Balawal Sen, son of Dahi Sen; Keshu Sen, son of Balawal Sen; Madhu Sen, son of Kashu Sen; Sur Sen, son of Madhu Sen; Bhim Sen, son of Sur Sen; Kanak Sen, son of Bhim Sen; Hari Sen, son of Kanak Sen; Ghan Sen, son of Hari Sen; Narain Sen, son of Ghan Sen; Lakhman Sen, son of Narain Sen; Madr Sen, son of Lakhman Sen.—xi. Raja Dip Singh. Six Rajas of this family ruled during 107 years and 7 months; Ran Singh, son of Dip Singh; Raj Singh, son of Ran Singh; Chatar Singh, son of Raj Singh; Nar Singh, son of Chatar Singh; Jiwan Singh, son of Nar Singh.—xii. Raja Pithaura. Of this line five princes filled the throne during 80 years 6 months and 10 days: Rai Abhai Mal, son of Rai Pithaura; Durjan Mal, son of Abhai

Mal; Udai Mal, son of Durjan Mal; Rai Vijai Mal, son of Udai Mal.

Part II.—History of the Muhammadan Emperors, from the reign of Shahabu-d din Ghori, who first ruled in Hindustan, to the thirteenth year of Shah 'Alam's reign, A.H. 1187 (1773 A.D.), a period of 635 years. This part is divided into nine Sections. [The author continues his list of contents in great detail.]

EXTRACTS

Khundi Rao, son of Malhar Rao, Mahratta, killed by Suraj Mal Jat; and Appaji Mahratta by the Rathor Rajputs

In 1160 A.H. (1747 A.D.) Appaji, Malhar Rao, and other Mahrattas, having collected a large force from Malwa and Gujarat, poured like a torrent upon Dig and Kumbher, then held by Suraj Mal Jat. They laid siege to those forts, and devastated the country. The war continued for several months, and ended in the death of Khandi Rao, who was killed in an action with Suraj Mal.

After the death of this chief, the Mahrattas, finding themselves unable to stand against the Jats, turned their arms towards the country of Raja Bakht Singh and other Rathor chiefs, and demanded a contribution from the Raja, who, immediately on receiving the massage, assembled a council of war, and thus resolutely addressed all his chiefs: "Alas! how deplorable is the condition of Rajputs, that a mean and contemptible tribe from the Dakhin demands tribute from them! Where are those Rajputs gone who were so brave, that only ten of them could oppose a thousand of the enemy, and who once with the edge of their sword not only punished the rebels who occupied the most secure and impenetrable valleys of Kabul, but drove them out and became masters of their strongholds? While the Rajputs occupied the road between Kabul and India, no power could force its way into this country from that direction, nor did any people there dare to disturb the peace of the subjects or rise in rebellion against the throne. Surely, the blood of true Rajputs is altogether extinct." He uttered many such inflammatory sentences before the assembly, and a Rajput, roused by his speech, broke silence and said, "The Rajputs of this time possess more courage than those of former ages; but the Rajas of the present time are not so brave or so judicious in command as they were of old." "Of course," replied the Raja, "if the soldiers of an army be cowards, blame is thrown upon the weakness and inability of its leader."

In short, after a long discussion, the Rajput rose up with six other persons, two of whom were his sons, two his nephews, and two his friends. They all mounted their horses, and spurring them on, proceeded direct to Appaji's camp, which was at the distance of thirty *kos* from that of Raja Bakht Singh. They alighted from their horses, and at once entered the tent of Appaji, turning a deaf ear to the guards who stood at the door and tried to prevent them from going in. The chief of these brave Rajputs, dauntlessly approaching the Mahratta chief, sat close to his cushion, and freely entered into a conversation with him. He asked him, in the name of his Raja, what he meant by coming into this territory, and demanding contribution from the Rathor chief. "I came here," replied Appaji, "by the force of my arms, and I demand the tribute by right of might. If God pleases, I will penetrate in a few days to the very palaces of your Raja." "No, no," said the Rajput, "you must not be too sure of your bravery and power. God has made other men stronger than you."

On hearing these words, Appaji's indignation knew no bounds, and at once breaking out into passion, he began to abuse him and the Raja. The Rajput could not restrain himself, and, inflamed with anger, drew out his dagger, and stabbing the Mahratta chief, put an end to his existence with one blow. Having severed his head from his body, he made off with it, and took it to Raja Bakht Singh, while his other companions engaged with the Mahrattas, who, with loud shouts, ran towards them, to avenge the death of their chief. Three of these Rajputs were slain, and three, though much wounded, escaped from the hands of the enemy. After the death of Appaji, the Mahrattas were obliged to decamp, and return to their country.

Death of 'Aliwardi Khan, Nazim of Bengal

'Aliwardi Khan, the Governor of Bengal, Maksudabad and Patna, having no son, and seeing that his end was fast approaching, appointed his daughter's son as his successor, and enjoined on him the observance of two precepts. First, that he should never enter into hostilities with the English. Secondly, that he should never exalt Ja'far 'Ali Khan to any great rank, or entrust him with such power as to involve himself in difficulty, in case of his revolt.

Siraju-d daula, however, soon forgot these precepts, and when, after the death of 'Aliwardi Khan, he succeeded to power, he took Ja'far 'Ali Khan into his favour, and conferred on him a *jagir*, to which he also attached a troop of horse and foot, and placed his whole army under his command. The English at Calcutta punctually paid their annual tribute, according to the fixed rate. But Siraju-d daula, through his covetousness and pride of power, demanded an increase of tribute from them, and became openly hostile towards them. Actuated by his vanity and presumption, he suddenly attacked them in Calcutta, and having plundered their property and cash, put several of their officers to death, and returned to Murshidabad.

As the English had taken no heed of his movements, they could not oppose him at the time with success; but afterwards they collected a large army, and marched boldly towards Murshidabad. They also brought over Ja'far 'Ali Khan to their interest, upon the promise of making over the province of Bengal to him. When their army reached within one or two marches from Murshidabad, Siraju-d daula advanced to oppose them. Ja'far 'Ali Khan, who had the command of all his forces, wished to capture and surrender him to the English without any battle being fought; but Siraju-d daula soon became acquainted with his intentions, and seeing himself in a helpless situation, secretly embarked alone in a boat and fled.

After his flight the English assigned the province of Bengal to Ja'far 'Ali Khan, who established his rule there, and appointed his deputies in all its districts. All the property of Siraju-d daula was taken and divided between him and the English. When Siraju-d daula had gone thirty *kos* from Murshidabad, he stopped for a while, and ordered his servant to land in the jungle, and try to get some fire for his *hukka*. Accordingly the servant disembarked, and seeing the cottage of a *darwesh*, he approached it, and asked the occupant for some fire.

It is said that the *darwesh* had been a servant of Siraju-d daula, and, being ignominiously turned out by him for some fault, he had become a *fakir*, and taken up his abode in this jungle. When he saw the servant of Siraju-d daula, with a *chillam* in his hand studded with gems, he instantly recognized him, and asked him how he happened to be there. The servant, who was a simpleton, discovered the whole matter to him; and the *darwesh*, quietly leaving him there, went with all speed to the governor of the neighbouring town, and informed him of Siraju-d daula's arrival. As orders for capturing the Nawab had been issued by Ja'far 'Ali Khan and the English, and the governor had received them on the same day, he immediately embarked on a boat, and, having seized the Nawab, sent him under the custody of some trusty servants to Ja'far 'Ali Khan, who put him to death in A.H. 1160 (1747 A.D.).

Having so far gratified his ambition, Ja'far 'Ali Khan with a settled mind devoted his attention to the management of Bengal, and took possession of all the wealth, and royal equipage of Siraju-d daula, who had involved himself in this danger by not observing the wise advice of his grandfather.

Safdar Jang and Suraj Mal Jat

When Safdar Jang was appointed chief minister by Ahmad Shah, the districts which, according to the established custom, comprised the *jagir* of a minister, were also granted to him. Faridabad, which is twelve *kos* distance from Shah-Jahanabad, had been formerly a part of this *jagir*; but since the time of the late minister, I'timadu-d daula, Balram, a near relation of Suraj Mal Jat, having put the officers of the minister to death, had made himself master of this district, and gave him only what he liked out of its revenues. The magnanimous spirit of Safdar Jang could not brook this usage, and he demanded in strong terms the surrender of the district by Suraj Mal Jat and Balram; but they still retained it, and answered him evasively.

At last, in A.H. 1160 (1747 A.D.), he marched to Dahli to punish them for their delay, and soon recovered Faridabad from Balram. Having pitched his tents there, he also demanded that Suraj Mal should resign all the places which belonged to the Emperor; but the Jat chief, on receiving this demand, began to fortify his posts of Dig, Kumbher and other places with strong garrisons, guns, and all the munitions of war, and having prepared himself for an engagement, addressed the minister sometimes with promises of surrender and sometimes with threats of vengeance.

Fight between Kaim Khan and Sa'du-llah Khan

In 1162 A.H. (1749 A.D.), when Safdar Jang was

endeavouring to recover possession of the districts which belonged to the Emperor, a misunderstanding arose arose between Kaim Khan, etc., the sons of Muhammad Bangash Afghan, and Sa'du-llah Khan and other sons of 'Ali Muhammad Khan Rohilla; and the two parties, the Afghans and the Rohillas, went so far in their animosity towards each other that they both had recourse to arms. Many battles took place between them, and at last the contest ended in the destruction of Kaim Khan, the eldest son of Muhammad Khan Bangash. The Afghans, after the death of their chief, took to flight; and the Rohillas returned victorious to their homes.

When the news of Kaim Khan's death became known, Safdar Jang left the matter with Suraj Mal Jat unsettled, and immediately came to Dehli. With the permission of the Emperor, he soon marched to Farrukhabad, the residence of Kaim Khan, and confiscated all the property of the Afghans, leaving only a few villages sufficient for the maintenance of Ahmad Khan and the other sons and relatives of Muhammad Khan. He placed the estates of the Afghans under the management of Raja Nuwul Rai, who acted as the Nawab's deputy in the governorship of the province of Oudh and Allahabad, and himself returned to Dehli.

Ja'far 'Ali Khan and Kasim 'Ali Khan

Ja'far 'Ali Khan, who had joined with the English, put Siraju-d daula, his sister's son, who governed Murshidabad, to death, and himself became governor of the province. Kasim 'Ali Khan, who was one of his near relations, acquired great strength, and collected a large force on the strength of his connexion with the governor. Miran, son of Ja'far 'Ali Khan, became deputy of his father, and, having assembled a large army, engaged in managing the affairs of the provinces. He resolved on punishing Khadim Husain Khan, governor of Puraniya, who refused submission to Ja'far

'Ali Khan. Having marched from Maksudabad, he reached the banks of the river which flows on the other side of Puraniya, and pitched his tents there. After a bridge of boats was made, Miran determined to cross the river next morning, and make a sudden attack upon Khadim Husain Khan. As he had collected a very large army, and was himself exceedingly bold and enterprising, Khadim Husain Khan was greatly alarmed, and prepared to escape during the night, leaving the city of Puraniya to the invader. But, accidentally, about the middle of the night, Miran, who was sleeping in his tent, was struck dead by lightning. When his army was left without a leader, many fled away for fear of Khadim Husain Khan, and the rest, with the camp, returned to Ja'far 'Ali Khan at Murshidabad. It is said that Miran was very generous. One day [having had no occasion to bestow alms] he said, "Some evil is about to befall me," and the same night he was struck by lightning and died.

Ja'far 'Ali Khan, after Miran's death, became weak and embarrassed. Kasim 'Ali Khan, his son-in-law, who through his kindness had been enabled to obtain power, and collect an army, joined with the English, and having invited them from Calcutta, took Ja'far 'Ali Khan prisoner. The English made Kasim 'Ali Khan governor of Bengal and 'Azimabad Patna, instead of Ja'far 'Ali Khan in 1170 A.H.

Shah 'Alam proceeds against Kalinjar

His Majesty, the asylum of the world, Shah 'Alam Badshah, having subdued the Deputy Subadar of the province of 'Azimabad, and taken a contribution from him, returned to the province of Oudh, which belonged to Nawab Shuja'u-d daula. The Nawab advanced to receive him with honour. The Emperor, accompanied by him, went towards Jhansi and the fort of Kalinjar, which were very strong places, and in the possession of the Bundela Rajas and Mahrattas. Shuja'd daula with his army went as far as Mahoba, which is near the fort of Kalinjar, and overran the country. The Raja of Kalinjar was obliged to pay him a contribution and also to promise an annual tribute.

The districts of Jhansi, Kalpi, etc., which belonged to the Bundelas and others, were after many battles and struggles taken from them, and annexed to the dominions of the Emperor and Nawab Shuja'u-d daula. . . . Afterwards they crossed the Ganges, and proceeded to Mahdighat, where they encamped in 1177 A.H. (1763 A.D.).

Kasim 'Ali Khan invites Shah 'Alam and Nawab Shuja'u-d daula to 'Azimabad, and a battle is fought with the English

When Kasim 'Ali Khan, Governor of the province of Bengal, Maksudabad and 'Azimabad Patna, having fled from the English, reached the vicinity of Benares, which belonged to Shuja'u-d daula, Shah 'Alam and the Nawab were encamped on the banks of the Jumna, at the *ghat* of Bibipur, within the boundary of Karra, to settle terms about the fort of Kalinjar, and correspondence was going on about the matter with Raja Hindupat. At that place a petition was received by the Emperor and a letter by the Nawab from Kasim 'Ali Khan, soliciting an interview, and requesting assistance, with promises of remuneration. Satisfactory replies were sent on the part of the Emperor and the Nawab. Kasim 'Ali Khan therefore left Benares, and when he arrived at the *ghat* of Bibipur, pitched his tents near the royal camp.

After an interview with the Emperor and Nawab Shuja'u-d daula, he presented them with a large donation in cash, valuables and curiosities, and derived encouragement and consolation from them. But as in those days a question was under dispute with Raja Hindupat, the Emperor and the Nawab could not attend to any other matter till that was settled. Kasim 'Ali

Khan, seeing that the Raja would not come to amicable terms, and that the Emperor and the Nawab could not go to 'Azimabad and Bengal until the dispute was adjusted, offered his mediation, and after an interview with the Raja, settled the question. A part of the contribution money, which the Raja had become liable to pay, was realized and for the remainder Kasim 'Ali Khan became surety. After this, he entreated the Emperor and the Nawab for assistance, and represented his desperate circumstances to them. He also promised to pay monthly all the expenses of their armies, till such time as he might obtain victory over the English, and reinstate himself in the provinces of Bengal and 'Azimabad.

Though some say that the Emperor did not wish to engage in hostilities, nevertheless it was at last determined that the provinces of Bengal and 'Azimabad should be taken from the English and given to Kasim 'Ali Khan, and also that the English should be punished. Accordingly, on the 1st of Zi-l ka'da, 1178 A.H. (20th April, 1765 A.D.),[1] the Emperor, Shuja'u-d daula Waziru-l Mamalik and Kasim 'Ali Khan marched towards 'Azimabad, as far as Benares. The English who were at 'Azimabad Patna trembled like an aspen at the fear of His Majesty Shah 'Alam Badshah and Nawab Shuja'u-d daula, and they sent petitions to them, soliciting forgiveness for their conduct. They deputed Shitab Rai on their part, promising to give up 'Azimabad, pay whatever might be demanded as a contribution, and obey any orders that might be given, praying also that the Emperor and the Nawab would return from Benares without attacking them.

The request of the English was not acceded to, Shitab Rai was turned out of the camp, and the royal army marched on from Benares. The English, being

[1][*This is a year too late. The real date is 3rd May, 1764.*]

informed of this, left the city of Patna, and having assembled at Bach Pahari, six *kos* from that city, on the road to Benares, fixed their batteries there. Relying upon destiny, they resolved to offer opposition, and prepared to fight.

The Emperor and the Nawab, having marched from Benares, proceeded by rapid marches, like an arrow shot from a bow, and encamped at five *kos* from Bach Pahari. The action commenced with the shooting of arrows and firing of muskets, and it continued for two days. The third day the brave and bold warriors of Shuja'u-d daula's army, making a vigorous attack, advanced their batteries close to Pahari, and engaged with the English, who also spared no effort in resistance, and exerted themselves to fight.

The whole day the warriors of both sides stood firm fighting in the field. At the close of the day, when the sun approached the horizon, the brave soldiers of both parties ceased to combat, and the batteries remained fixed in their first positions. But Shuja'u-d daula, by the advice of some ignorant and inexperienced men who were with him, recalled the warriors of his army from Pahari to his own tents. Although Shuja' Kuli Khan and others who were at the batteries remonstrated with him, and remarked that to remove them from their position would be highly inexpedient, because they had been fixed there with great difficulty and pains, and in case of retreat it would be very difficult to regain the position, yet the Nawab would not listen to them, and having recalled the soldiers from Pahari, ordered the batteries to be fixed near his camp.

The English, considering this a favour of God, occupied the position where the batteries of the enemy had been. The next day the Nawab could not drive the English from it. In these same days, the wet season commenced, and rain began to fall. The place where the tents of the Emperor and Shuja'u-d daula were pitched being low, and water having collected there, it was considered unfit for the camp, and His Majesty and the Nawab retreated to Baksar, which is thirty *kos* east of Benares. When the rains were over, in consequence of the war having been prolonged for several months, and the collection of the revenues from the provinces which belonged to Shuja'u-d daula having been delayed on account of the expedition, and as the army which was newly enlisted by the Emperor and the Nawab for this war with the English, as well as the veteran troops, began to demand their pay, the Emperor and the Nawab asked Kasim 'Ali Khan for the money which he had promised for the expenses of the army. But he evaded payment by frivolous excuses. As the demand for arrears created a mutinous spirit in the army, and as Kasim 'Ali Khan, notwithstanding that he was importuned and entreated to pay the money, would not come to a right understanding, but resorted to unfair and dishonest expedients, the Emperor and the Nawab took harsh measures against him, and having called him from his tent, put him under the custody of a guard. Whatever property of his they could lay their hands on, such as elephants and horses, they sold, and paid the army from the proceeds.

When the rainy season was over, the English, having marched from 'Azimabad, pitched their tents near Baksar, opposite the Emperor's and the Nawab's camp, at a distance of five or six *kos*. Lines of intrenchment were prepared on either side, and the action commenced with guns and muskets. As Nawab Shuja'u-d daula had heavy artillery with him, the English army could not stand against it, and they at last prepared to engage in close combat. When recourse was had to this kind of warfare, both parties stood their ground firmly, and the warriors of both sides, expertly using their swords, bows and arrows, destroyed their opponents, and increased the business in the market of the angel of death. The brave and intrepid warriors of Nawab Shuja'u-d daula's army, having overcome the enemy, fell upon his camp, and stretched out their hands to plunder. They put a great number of them to the sword, and beat the drums of triumph and conquest. The Nawab ordered his soldiers not to let any one escape alive. The army of Shuja'u-d daula surrounded the enemy on all sides, and the English, having no way left for flight, collected at one spot, and having resolved to die, made a very desperate attack upon their opponents. Shuja' Kuli Khan, *alias* 'Isa, who was a slave of the Nawab, and had 4000 horse under his command, observed the furious attack of the English, and cried out to his soldiers, "Friends! it was for such a day as this that you put on those arms. Form a compact body, and at once charge the enemy, and put them to the sword." His followers seemed ready to obey the command. They read the *fatiha*, and filled up their hands in prayer. 'Isa, thinking that they would follow him, galloped his horse towards the English front, but only five horsemen out of four thousand followed him. Of those cowards who remained behind, some took to flight, and others stood idle on their ground. 'Isa with his drawn sword furiously attacked the enemy like a Rustam. He killed many, and after astonishing feats of valour, drank the cup of martyrdom. Having shown his loyalty, he met with the mercy of God.

When Shuja' Kuli Khan, *alias* 'Isa, was slain, all his cavalry at once took to flight, and caused great confusion in the army of Nawab Shuja'u-d daula. The English, being informed of this, with great impetuosity attacked the division of Raja Beni Bahadur, the deputy of the Nawab. The Raja, who had never been in action, could not stand his ground, and fled without attempting to fight. As he commanded several thousands, both of horse and foot, his flight caused the defeat of the armies of the Emperor and the Nawab. The English took possession of the intrenchments of the fugitives. Although the Nawab tried much to rally them, and cried out (in the words of Sa'di), "Ye brave men, exert yourselves to fight, and do not put on the clothes of women," yet none returned, all sought safety in flight.

When the Nawab and the Emperor's forces fled, the English fell upon their camps, and began to plunder them. The Nawab hastened in confusion towards Benares, and halted when he arrived there. The English took possession of his tents, guns and other property. The Emperor also fled to Benares. The Nawab, after some days, hastened to Allahabad, and stayed there three months collecting a large army.

The English, in the mean time, laid siege to Chunar. Sidi Muhammad Bashir Khan, the Governor, offered opposition, and, opening his artillery from the ramparts, fought very bravely. But when several days had passed, and nobody came to reinforce him (for the fort was near Benares, and the Nawab was at Allahabad), he was obliged to capitulate, and leave the fort in their possession. He was allowed to go to Nawab Shuja'u-d daula at Allahabad. The English made an alliance with Shah 'Alam, who was at Benares, and marched with him from that place to Jaunpur. The Nawab moved towards the same place at the head of a large army, with the intention of hazarding a battle.

Both parties encamped near Jaunpur, at the distance of two or three *kos* from each other, and skirmishes took place between them. Two or three English officers fell into the hands of the Mughals of the Nawab's army, and this obliged the English to propose terms of peace through the Mughal chiefs, who at their request advised the Nawab to accept the terms. Beni Bahadur, and some other short-sighted and ignorant people dissuaded him from liberating the English officers, and he would not agree to peace. This created enmity and disaffection in the minds of the Mughal chiefs against the Nawab, and they accordingly entered into an understanding with the English, that if they delivered the Nawab into the hands of the English on the day of battle, they should be rewarded with appointments in the provinces. The Nawab, being apprised of this, was greatly alarmed, because the Mughals were the most powerful body in his army. When the armies prepared to engage, the Mughals stood aloof, and as the Nawab's affairs were reduced to a desperate condition, and a battle could not be hazarded, he broke up his camp near Jaunpur, and retreated towards Lucknow.

When he reached that place, Simru[2] Gardi, who was at the head of ten or twelve thousand Gardi Telinga soldiers; Gusain Anup Gir, who commanded several thousand horse; and 'Ali Beg Khan, Shitab Jang, and Agha Bakir, who, though Mughals, had not joined with the insurgents, hastened to meet the Nawab. Najaf Khan, Muhammad 'Ali Khan, Agha Rahim and other Mughal chiefs, went over to the English, and the rest of the army fled.

On the 9th of Sha'ban, c.H. 1178 (1 Feb. 1765), the Nawab with his whole family, and all the property which he could collect, marched from Lucknow towards Bareilly, which belonged to Hafiz Rahmat Rohilla. On leaving Lucknow, the Nawab encamped at *baoli* (well), near Rustam-nagar.

Nawab Shuja'u-d daula, having reached Bareilly, which formed the *ta'luka* of Hafiz Rahmat Rohilla, left his family there with Simru Gardi, who was at the head of several thousand horse and foot soldiers. He himself proceeded to Garh Muktesar, which is situated on the banks of the Ganges, thirty *kos* from Shah-Jahanabad. He met there the chiefs of the Mahratta army, and made an alliance with them. Having returned thence, he came to Farrukhabad. Gusain Anup Gir, who was a great general and one of the oldest servants of the Nawab, quarrelled with him while encamped on the banks of the Ganges near Garh Muktesar, on account of the pay of his regiments, and having deserted him, went over to Jawahir Singh, son of Suraj Mal Jat.

[2]*[The adventurer "Sumroo" or "Sombre."]*

When Nawab Shuja'u-d daula arrived at Farrukhabad, he requested Ahmad Khan and Muhammad Khan Bangash, Hafiz Rahmat, Dundi Khan, Najib Khan, and other Rohilla and Afghan chiefs, to lend him their aid; but through fear of the English they all refused to accompany him. Ghaziu-d din Khan 'Imadu-l Mulk, who was in those days with Ahmad Khan at Farrukhabad, accompanied Shuja'u-d daula from Farrukhabad to the Mahrattas at Kora. The Mahrattas went with them to the ferry of Jajmau, on the banks of the Ganges. The English left Allahabad, and came to the same place, when Nawab Shuja'u-d daula, Ghaziu-d din Khan and the Mahrattas resolved to oppose them.

After an obstinate battle, the army of the Mahrattas took to flight, and having plundered on their way the city of Kora, arrived at Kalpi. Ghaziu-d din, with a few men, fled to Farrukhabad. Shuja'u-d daula, disappointed in obtaining help and assistance in every quarter, determined to venture alone to the English, and make peace with them, rather than wander from place to place in a state of embarrassment. He accordingly came unattended to Jajmau, where the English had encamped. When he approached the camp, and the English were informed of his coming, their chiefs, who were very polite and affable, immediately came out of their tents, and proceeded on foot to meet him. They showed him great hospitality and respect, and, accompanying him to their tents with due honour, promised to restore to him the provinces which had been in his possession, and told him that he was at liberty to place his family wherever he liked. The Nawab, having taken his leave from the English, pitched his tents at the distance of four *kos* from theirs. He summoned his family from Bareilly, and sent them to Lucknow.

Simru, commander of the Gardi regiment, who was now in the service and in charge of the Nawab, had been formerly in the employ of the English; and, taking some offence at them, had entered the service of

Kasim 'Ali Khan, Governor of Bengal, and when the Khan was ruined, had entered at Baksar into the service of Nawab Shuja'u-d daula. As peace was now made, the English demanded his surrender by the Nawab; but the Nawab, respecting his bravery and courage, did not consider it proper to comply, but dismissed Simru from his service. Simru, who was coming with the family of the Nawab from Bareilly to Lucknow, learnt the news of his dismissal on the way. On this he petitioned for the arrears of his pay, and resolved to take severe measures in the event of refusal. The Nawab Begam, mother of Nawab Shuja'u-d daula, and Beni Bahadur, paid him what was due to him near Shahabad, and then dismissed him. Having received his pay, he went to Jawahir Singh Jat at Dig and Kumbher. The family of the Nawab, with the Khanam Sahiba and others, arrived at the *baoli* (well), near Lucknow, on the 9th Muharram A.H. 1179 (28 June, 1765 A.D.), and pitched their tents there.

As by this time the Nawab, in company with the English, had reached Phuphamau, near Allahabad; his family followed him to the same place. But the English intimated to him that he should leave the ladies of his family at Faizabad, and himself accompany them to Maksudabad, where their chief resided. The Nawab acted according to their request, and, having embarked in a boat, accompanied them to that city by water, with only a few attendants. When an interview took place between the English and the Nawab on the way between 'Azimabad and Maksudabad, they showed him great hospitality and kindness, and wrote him a letter, in which they restored to him both the provinces which had been in his possession. They took from him the district of Allahabad, with several other *mahals*, the annual revenue of which amounted altogether to twelve *lacs* of rupees, and also the district of Kora, and they gave these places to Shah 'Alam Badshah. They also promised to pay the Emperor annually a sum of fifty *lacs* of rupees on account

of the provices of Bengal and 'Azimabad, and having placed their officers in the fort of Allahabad, they erected a factory there. From the 13th of Rabi'u-l awwal, A.H. 1179, the Nawab's rule was again established in the provinces of Oudh and Allahabad.[1] The Emperor took up his residence in Sultan Khusru's garden at Allahabad. The English garrisoned the fort of Allahabad, and erected a factory in Benares. Hooper was appointed Resident at the Court of the Nawab.

The English

How can I sufficiently extol the courage, generosity, and justice of the English? In bravery Rustam cannot be compared to them, because, with only 10,000 foot soldiers, they marched from Maksudabad to 'Azimabad, fighting against the army of Kasim 'Ali Khan, consisting of 100,000 horse and foot, and never showed their backs in battle. In the same manner they engaged four times with the armies of Shuja'u-d daula and the Emperor, which amounted to more than 100,000 infantry and horse, and yet never retreated from the field. Moreover, they have fought against the Mahrattas and Ghaziu-d din Khan, and always with a similar result. Hatim Tai, who is said to have been the very model of generosity, had not perhaps such a liberal mind and magnanimous spirit as they have, because; after obtaining victory over Siraju-d daula, they gave the provinves of Bengal and 'Azimabad to Ja'far Ali Khan, and afterwards to Kasim 'Ali Khan, and after conquering the provinces of Oudh and Allahabad, they restored them both to Nawab Shuja'u-d daula. Naushirwan is mentioned as most just and equitable, but in justice and equity the English are not inferior to him. When they entered the city of Lucknow, and other cities and towns in the provinces of Oudh and Allahabad, as conquerors,

[1] [*Allahabad was not restored, but, as stated above, was given to the Emperor.*]

they did not hurt there even an ant, and in no way injured or troubled any person. Notwithstanding that many turbulent and seditious characters instigated them, and pointed out to them the riches of the people, told them that certain bankers possessed great wealth, and urged that it should be exacted from them, yet these righteous people allowed no mischief to be done, but on the contrary, punished these low informers, and cautioned them against spelling such words again. They strictly ordered their soldiers to commit no act of oppression or extortion upon any individual. Hooper was long a Resident at the Court of Nawab Shuja'u-d daula, and yet, during the period of seven or eight years he was so accredited, neither he himself nor any of his servants committed a single act of violence against any person. Monsieur Laintin (?), a Firingi, who was one of the greatest of Nawab Shuja'u-d daula's followers, conducted himself in the same exemplary manner; and although he sent Syam Lal, his *diwan*, to prison at the instigation of *diwan's* enemies, still he gave him no unnecessary pain. In short, the goodness of these people is beyond all bounds, and it is on account of their own and their servants' honesty that they are so fortunate and wealthy.

Jawahir Singh and Ratan Singh, sons of Suraj Mal Jat, and their successors

In the month of Jumada-s sani, 1181 A.H. (Oct. 1767), Jawahir Singh, son of Suraj Mal Jat, marched from Dig and Kumbher, which were his residences, to bathe in the tank of Pokhar, a great sacred place of the Hindus. It is situated near Ajmir, within the territory of Raja Madhav Singh, son of Raj Jai Singh Kachhwaha; and Jawahir Singh, on reaching the boundary of the Raja's possessions, began to ravage the country and plundered the people. He overran most places in the territory. When he reached within two stages from Pokhar, he learnt that Raja Bijai Singh, son of Raja Bakht Singh Rathor, had also come to bathe. Fearing on account of the outrages he had committed on his way, he wrote to Bijai Singh that he was suspicious of Madhu Singh, and that, if he would permit him, he would come to bathe. The Raja wrote in reply that he should come only with 2000 horse; but Jawahir Singh, contrary to this desire, proceeded with all his forces, which consisted of about 60,00 horse, one lac of foot, and one thousand large and small guns. On the 13th of Jumada-s sani, he bathed in the tank, and having halted a few days there, returned.

The news of his outrages and plundering having reached Madhu Singh and other Rajput chiefs, they considered it a great insult, and contrary to custom. All the Rajputs havings assembled together, went to Madhu Singh . . . proposing to take revenge. Madhu Singh replied that he did not think it worthy of himself to oppose Jawahir Singh, whose forefathers had been of the lowest dependents and creatures of his ancestors, but that whosoever liked might go against him. Accordingly Dalel Singh and other Rajputs, to the number of about 20,000 horse, and an equal body of foot soldiers, went to oppose Jawahir Singh, who, finding it difficult to force his way, resolved to fight. A battle ensued. The Rajputs showed such bravery and courage, that they destroyed about 20,000 horse and foot of the army of Jawahir Singh. Many also drank the cup of death on their part. Jawahir Singh, not being able to stand before the cruel sword of the Rajputs, took to flight alone, and with great difficulty and pain reached Dig and Kumbher. His guns, elephants, horses, treasure, and all the furniture of pomp, fell into the hands of the Rajputs, who, after staying a few days on the field, returned to their respective residences.

Jawahir Singh felt great shame of this defeat, and much of the vanity and pride which he had entertained was reduced. It is said that Jawahir Singh had made a soldier his associate and had great frendship for him.

This soldier, having been guilty of some improper act, was disgraced. . . . One day, when the Jat chief had gone hunting with only a few attendants, that soldier, taking his sword and chield, went to the place where Jawahir Singh was standing carelessly with a few men, and struck him a blow with his sword, saying, "This is the punishment of the disgrace I have received." In one blow there was an end of Jawahir Singh's existence, who departed to the world of eternity in the month of Safar, 1182 A.H. (June, 1768 A.H.). He was succeeded by his brother Ratan Singh. . . .

When Ratan Singh was killed by a *fakir*, the ministers of the State elevated his infant son, Ranjit Singh, to his place, and seated him upon the *masnad* of the chiefship. Nuwul Singh and Bhawani Singh, sons of Suraj Mal, but by another wife, rose in opposition, and collected an army of Mahrattas and others, to the number of about 30,000 horse, and an equal number of foot soldiers. The ministers of Ranjit called the Sikh forces from Lahore. These forces then entered the territories of the Jat, and stretched out their hands to plunder. Although the Jats opposed them, yet they did not withhold their hands. At last, the armies of Ranjit Singh, being collected, fought with the Sikhs, and drove them out of his possessions. Nuwul Singh and Bhawani Singh went with the Mahratta army towards Malwa and Ujjain. The son of Ballu Jat, who had raised a rebellion in the territory, and wished to alienate a part from it, and make himself its master, was also baffled in his schemes, and could not succeed in his objects.

In the month of Safar, 1183 A.H. (June, 1769 A.D.), the town of Dig Kumbher twice caught fire, and about twelve or thirteen thousand men were burnt. No account was taken of the animals and houses which were consumed.

In the same year Tukkaji Holkar, son-in-law[4] of Malhar Rao, Ram Chand Ganesh and other Mahrattas

[4] *He was "no way related to Malhar Rao".— Malcolm's "Central India", vol. i. p. 169; Grant Duff, vol. ii. p. 196.*

proceeded with a formidable army of one *lac* of horse and foot from the Dakhin, and reached the territory of Ranjit Singh. A great conflict took place between the Jat and Mahratta forces, and numerous men on both sides fell in the field. But the gale of victory blew in favour of the Mahratta army, and the Jats took refuge in the most fortified of their strongholds. The Mahratta army overran and spread devastation in the country which belonged to Ranjit Singh Jat, from Agra to Kol and Jalesar. The Jats, having assembled their forces, prepared to oppose them, and at last peace was made between the parties. The Jats gave a contribution of about forty-five *lacs* of rupees to the Mahrattas, and saved the country from their depredations. Being restored to their possessions, they banished the fear of the Mahrattas from their minds. Civil feuds had broken out among Nuwul Singh, Ranjit Singh, and other sons and grandsons of Suraj Mal Jat, and great disturbances took place, in consequence.

Najaf Khan, in the commencement of the year 1187 A.H. (1173 A.D.), made an irruption into the territories of the Jats; the Biluchis, Mewattis, and other tribes also joined with him. He brought many places which belonged to them into his possession, and has continued to spread disturbances in their territories up to this day, the 9th of Jumada-s sani, 1189 A.H. (August 1775 A.D.). He subdued the Jats, and reduced the Rajas to subjection, as we have particularized in the chapter which gives his history. Najaf Khan took the fortress of Dig by storm from the Jats, who according to some, also lost possession of Kumbher. This place, as well as Agra, Mathura, Brindaban, Kol, Jalesar and Kama, besides many other *mahals*, fell into the possession of Najaf Khan, who at the present day, the 1st of the month of Jumada-l awwal, 1192 A.H. (1 June, 1778 A.D.), has been engaged for some time in besieging the fort of Machehri.

Account of Bengal, Maksudabad, and Patna 'Azimabad, and of the cities of Calcutta and Dacca

When the English had driven out Kasim 'Ali Khan from Bengal, Maksudabad and 'Azimabad Patna, they confirmed the son of Ja'far 'Ali Khan in the deputy-governorship of Bengal, and Shitab Rai in that of 'Azimabad Patna. The armies which were stationed in those provinces under the command of the former governors were all dismissed, and the necessary number of Telinga *barkandazes* were enlisted, to be kept at the disposal of the deputy-governors of the provinces. It is said that a very strange practice was introduced into the country, namely, that the English began to sell some articles themselves, and that they prohibited other traders from dealing in them according to former practice.

In the month of Shawwal, 1183 A.H. (February 1770 A.D.), in the city of Calcutta, where the English resided, such a storm raged that many men were killed, and houses destroyed by the force of the hurricane. In the same year such a dreadful famine occurred in Calcutta, Bengal, and 'Azimabad, that in places where four *maunds* of grain had been sold for a rupee, even four *sirs* were not then to be obtained for the same money. Consequently many persons died of hunger. It is said that in Bengal and 'Azimabad about three million seven hundred thousand men were starved to death; and many sold their sons and daughters for grain, or for four or eight *annas* a piece. On account of this dearth, the English sent several hundred boats from Calcutta to Faizabad for the purpose of procuring grain. Thus the price of corn was also raised in Faizabad and Lucknow.

It is said that in the month of Muharram, 1183 A.H. (May 1769 A.D.), such showers of hailstones fell, that the whole city of Calcutta where the English resided, was reduced to ruins. Several men were killed, houses levelled to the ground, and only a few men survived.

In the same month and the same year hailstones fell also in the city of Maksudabad.

It is said that the English are so just and honest, that they do not interfere with the wealth of any rich men, bankers, merchants and other people who reside in their cities, but, on the contrary, they are very kind to those who are wealthy. But from those who are powerful they manage to obtain money by their wisdom and adroitness, and even by force if necessary; but they are not oppressive, and never trouble poor people....

Arrival of Governor Hastings at Lucknow

When, in 1198 A.H. (1784 A.D.), the news spread in Faizabad, Lucknow, and other places under the jurisdiction of the Nawab Waziru-l Mamalik Asafu-d daula, ruler of the provinces of Oudh and Allahabad, that the Governor General, Hastings, was coming from Calcutta towards Lucknow, Nawab Asafu-d daula, with a view to welcome him, marched from that city on the 9th of Rabi'u-s sani, and encamped at Jhusi, near Allahabad. When the intelligence of the Governor General's arrival at Benares was received, the Nawab despatched the minister, Haidar Beg Khan, accompanied by Almas 'Ali Khan, Governor of Kora and Etawa, an officer of great ability and influence. They met the Governor General at Benares, and having presented their *nazars*, remained in attendance on him. When the Governor General reached Allahabad, Nawab Asafu-d daula crossed the river, and after an interview had taken place between these magnates, they came together to Lucknow. Great rejoicings were made by the people on account of the arrival of the Governor General, ...

Destruction of Pilgrims at Hardwar

Every year, in the month of Baisakh (April), the people of India, particularly Hindus, resort to Hardwar, a place of great sanctity, for the purpose of bathing, and a fair lasts for several days. It is said that in Jumada-l awwal, 1198 A.H. (April, 1748 A.D.) in the (Hindi) month of Baisakh, when the people had collected as usual, such a deadly blast arose that fifteen hundred persons, men and women, died from it in less than two hours. In the same month and year thousands of persons lost their lives from starvation in Dehli in a space of five or six days, on account of the dearth of corn. The famine raged from Multan down to Bengal and Maksudabad, with such violence that people were reduced to a very deplorable state. They laboured under double difficulties, one the scarcity of grain, and the other the want of employment, which equally affected both the soldier and the tradesman.

Hastings, Governor General, imprisoned and sent home by orders of the King of England[a]

Hastings, who some years previously had been appointed by the King of England as Governor of Bengal, Maksudabad, and 'Azimabad Patna, revolted from his obedience, and paid no attention to the King's orders, declaring that he was a servant of the Kings of India.[b] The King of England sent another governor to Calcutta in his place; and when he arrived in Calcutta, and went to visit Hastings, that gentleman killed him by the power of his sorceries.

After this, the King of England despatched another officer to fill the place of Hastings at Calcutta; but that gentleman declined to resign charge of the government. At last they determined on fighting a duel, with the understanding that the victor should assume the office of Governor. A day was fixed, and on that day they fought a duel. Hastings escaped, but wounded his antagonist in the arm with a pistol-ball, who was consequently obliged to return to England.

[a] [This short Extract has been retained, not for its accuracy, but for its Indian view of the subject.]

[b] [The Directors of the East India Company.]

The King of England then contrived a plot and sent to Calcutta about four hundred European soldiers, in a vessel under the command of Macpherson, with a letter to Hastings, to the effect that, as in these days he had many battles to fight, Macpherson had been despatched with these soldiers to reinforce him, and to render service to him whenever exigency might require it. Secret instructions were given to Macpherson and the soldiers to seize Hastings and forward him to His Majesty's presence. When the ship reached near Calcutta, Macpherson sent the Royal letter to Hastings, and saluted him with the fire of guns of the ship. Hastings, having read the letter, embarked in a boat, and, in company of the other English officers who were with him in Calcutta, proceeded to welcome Macpherson. On his approaching the vessel, Macpherson paid a salute, and with a double guard of the European soldiers, went from the ship into Hasting's boat. Immediately on boarding the boat, he ordered the soldiers to surround Hastings, and having thus made him a prisoner showed him the orders for his own appointment as Governor, and the warrant which His Majesty had given for the apprehension of Hastings, who saw no remedy but to surrender himself a prisoner. Macpherson sent him to England in a ship under the custody of the European guard which had come out for that purpose.

TARIKH-I SHADAT-I FARRUKH SIYAR

OF

MIRZA MUHAMMAD BAKHSH

[THE full title of this work is *Tarikh-i Shahadat-i Siyar wa Julus-i Muhammad Shah*. The author, Mirza Muhammad Bakhsh, was a poet, and wrote under the name Ashob. Nothing has been found about him beyond what he himself tells us in his Preface. He was a soldier and served with Nawab Mu'inu-l Mulk, "from the beginning to the end of the war with Ahmad Shah Abdali." He records how in this war he personally overthrew and granted quarter to three Abdali horsemen, for which exploit he obtained great applause and reward. Afterwards he served under Khan-khanan (Itizamu-d daula), and obtained a *mansab* of 200, with his ancestral title of Kaswar Khan; but he adds that this title was beyond his deserts, and he remained contented with his simple name of Muhammad Bakhsh. Subsequently he acted in company with 'Imadu-l Mulk Ghaziu-d din Khan. He seems to have been a bold dashing officer, and he had several brothers and friends serving with him. His name frequently appears in the course of the work when he records what he himself did or saw, as in the Extract which follows.

The work bears no special relation to the death of Farrukh Siyar. The author's intention was to write the history of "the hundred years from the death of Aurangzeb to the present time, 1196 A.H." (1782 A.D.); but Sir H. M. Elliot's MS. and another in the Library of the India Office close with the return of Nadir Shah, and the death of Zakariya Khan, governor of the Panjab. The history is very summary up to the beginning of the reign of Muhammad Shah, after which it is written in full detail. The author acknowledges his obligations to the *Tarikh-i Muhammad Shah*, but has also recorded "what he heared from trustworthy persons, and what he saw when serving Sultans and *wazirs*." In his Preface he mentions the works that he used for his Introduction. They are the usual authorities: the *Akbarnama*, *Tabakat-i Akbari*, *Ikbal-nama-i Jahangiri*, "the Journal which Jahangir himself wrote in a very pleasant style," and many other works. There are some references also to his own poetical productions—a poem of 270 couplets called *Falak-ashob*, written at Bhartpur, "one of the strong fortresses of Suraj Mal Jat," and another called *Kar-nama*, "Book of Deeds," in 5000 couplets, written by command to celebrate the wars of Nawab Mu'inu-l Mulk.

In the course of the Preface he speaks of the English in highly eulogistic terms. He specially mentions Captain Jonathan Scott, whose learning and acquirements he extols in verse, and for whose encouragement he is grateful. He also acknowledges the countenance and kindness which he received from Colonel Polier at Lucknow.

Size—9 inches by 8, 670 pages of 15 lines each.]

EXTRACT

[When Nizamu-l Mulk went forth to treat with Nadir Shah, the author of this work, with several horsemen consisting of his brethren and near relations, by the strength of their horses, but with great difficulty and much management, got in front of the elephants of Asaf Jah Nizamu-l Mulk, and arrived first at the battle-field. . . . As we were before all, we had the first sight. The Persians and others of Nadir's army, having dismounted and picketed their horses, were plundering and ransacking without check. They had broken open the chests with blows of axes and swords, torn in pieces the bags of gold and silver, and having scattered the contents on the ground, were engaged in picking them up. Furniture, especially the culinary utensils of silver and copper, fell into the hands of the plunderers.

When we reached the place of meeting, it was dark, and every one, great and small, remained on the spot he first reached. His Majesty approached with a large escort of men and guns with great splendour. Next came the train of the chief *wazir* 'Azimu-llah Khan Zahiru-d daula Bahadur. His elephant was in armour, and he himself rode in an iron *howda*, and was clothed in armour from head to foot, so that his eyes were the only parts of his body that were visible. He was attended by a suitable escort of men and arms, and made his obeisance to his monarch, and his *salam* to Asaf Jah. Next came the *Waziru-l mamalik* Bahadur. . . . All the chiefs were mounted on elephants clad in armour, in war *howdas* of iron variously ornamented, and all the elephant riders from the greatest to the least were covered with arms and armour from head to foot.]

WAKI'AT-I AZFARI

[This is one of the works mentioned by Sir H. M. Elliot as containing matter for the history of Shah 'Alam. He did not obtain a copy of the work, and all that is known about it is derived from a letter to Sir Henry by Sir Walter Elliot. It says, "The *Waki'at-i Azfari* is a mere autobiography of an individual of no note. This Azfari had some intercourse with Ghulam Kadir in his youth, and gives a few particulars of events which passed under his own observation." From the extracts inclosed in this letter it is apparent that the work was written after the death of Ghulam Kadir, which occurred in 1788 A.D.]

BAHRU-L MAWWAJ
OF
MUHAMMAD 'ALI KHAN ANSARI

The author of this work is Muhammad 'Ali Khan Ansari, Iban 'Izzatu-d daula Hidayatu-llah Khan, son of Shamsu-d daula Lutfu-llah Khan Sadik Tahawwur Jang.

Being devoted from his early youth, as most of these authors say of themselves, to history and studies subsidiary to it, and passing most of his time in the company of those who spoke and wrote of these subjects, he determined upon writing a general history; and as he had already written an account of the Prophets, he thought he could not do better than devote his time to a more secular History, embracing the lives of the Kings who in past times have ruled upon the earth; so that, through both his labourers combined, he might derive the double reward of hope of heaven and advantage upon earth. Relying, therefore, upon the help of God, he allowed "the parrot of his tongue to expatiate in the garden of language," and after spending a very long time upon his compilation, he completed it in the year 1209 A.H., corresponding with A.D. 1794-5.

It is a comprehensive and useful work, as will be seen from the list of contents given below, but it presents nothing particularly worthy of extract.

The work is divided into nine Chapters, and forty-nine Sections, fancifully called seas (*bahr*) and waves (*muj*) respectively, and hence the title of *Bahru-l Mawwaj*, "The Tempestuous Sea."

CONTENTS

Preface. p. 1.—Book I. In six Chapters: 1. Pashdadians; 2. Kaianians; 3. Tawaifu-l Muluk; 4. Sassanians; 5. Akasira; 6. Tubbas of Yemen, p. 8.—II. In two Chapters: 1. Ummayides; 2. 'Abbasides, p. 64.—III. In eleven Chapters: 1. Tahirians; 2. Saffarians; 3. Samanians; 4. Ghaznivides; 5. Ghorians; 6. Buwaihides; 7. Saljukians; 8. Khwarizmshahis; 9. Atabaks; 10. Isma'ilians; 11. Chiefs of Kara Khitai and Kirman, p. 112.—IV. In eight Chapters: 1. The Cæsars; 2. The Saljuks of Rum; 3. Danishmandias; 4. Salifias; 5. Manguchakias; 6. Rulers of Karaman; 7. Zulkadarias; 8. Othmanlis, p. 175.—V. On the Sharifs of Mecca and Medina, p. 208.—VI. In four Chapters: 1. Turk, the son of Yafath; 2. Tatar, and his descendants; 3. The Mughals; 4. Puranjar Kaan, p. 211. —VII. In seven Chapters, on Changiz Khan and his descendants, p. 219.—VIII. In five Chapters: 1. Chanbanians; 2. Ilkanians; 3. Muzaffarians; 4. Rulers of Kirit; 5. Saribarans, p. 274.—IX. In Six Chapters: 1. Timur and his descendants; 2. His descendants who ruled in Iran and Khurasan; 3. Kara-kuinlu Turks; 4. Ak-kuinlu; 5. Saffarians; 6. Nadir Shah, Ahmad Shah Abdali, etc., p. 319.

SIZE—Large 8vo., containing 437 pages, with 17 lines to a page.

This work is known to me only from a copy in the Library of the Raja of Benares, and I have never heard of any other. A ponderous commentary on the Kuran bears the same title.

'IBRAT-NAMA
OF
FAKIR KHAIRU-D DIN MUHAMMAD

[The author of this work was Fakir Khairu-d din Allahabadi, who also wrote the History of Jaunpur translated by Major Pogson and the *Balwant-nama*, to be hereafter noticed. During the latter part of his life he resided at Jaunpur, in the enjoyment of a pension from the British Government, which he had earned principally by the assistance which he rendered to Anderson in his negotiations with the Mahrattas. He left the service of Anderson through sickness, and was afterwards in the service of one of the Imperial princes. Subsequently he retired to Lucknow, and obtained some favour from the Nawab Sa'adat 'Ali, whom he greatly extols, and whose high sounding titles he recites in full as "I'timadu-d daulat wau-d din I'tizadu-l Islam wau-l Muslimin Waziru-l 'Umdatu-l Mulk Yaminu-d daulat Nazimu-l Mulk Nawab Sa'adat 'Ali Khan Bahadur Mubariz Jang." The author died about the year 1827.

The work may be considered as a History of the reigns of 'Alamgir II. and Shah 'Alam, for although it begins with Timur, the lives of the Emperors before 'Alamgir are dismissed in a very summary way, and occupy altogether only 25 pages. The main portion of the work, the reign of Shah 'Alam especially, is very full and minute, and the author shows himself particularly well acquainted with the affairs of Sindhia. The work is of considerable length, and is divided into years and many chapters. It closes soon after recounting the horrible cruelties practised on the Emperor Shah 'Alam and his family by the infamous Ghulam Kadir, whose atrocities he describes at length, and whose conduct he denounces in the strongest language: "The greatest of all the calamities that have fallen upon Hindustan were the acts of the traitor Ghulam Kadir, which deprived the Imperial house of all its honour and dignity, and consigned himself, his relations, and his tribe, to everlasting infamy."

A subsequent chapter describes the death of Ghulam Kadir, whose career induced the author to give his work the title of 'Ibrat-nama, "Book of Warning." It extends to 1204 A.H. (1790 A.D.), and was written before the end of the reign of Shah 'Alam. The history is well written, in simple intelligible language, and deserves more notice than the limits of this work will allow. Some Extracts follow, translated chiefly by the Editor, but a few passages are by munshis.

Sir H. Elliot's copy was bought at Lucknow, and is a folio 14 inches by 9, containing 500 pages of 25 lines to the page.]

EXTRACTS

Mutiny against 'Imadu-l Mulk Ghaziu-d din

['Imadu-l Mulk, after arranging the revenue and other matters (upon the accession of 'Alamgir II.), set about a reformation of the cavalry and *sin dagh*[1] system, which had fallen into a very corrupt state. He removed the Emperor from Shah-Jahanabad to Panipat, and then, taking away from the officials of the cavalry the lands which they held round the capital, he appointed his own officers to manage them. The chiefs of the cavalry, being hurt by the deprivation of their sources of income, and being encouraged by the Emperor and some of his councillors, were clamorous against the *wazir*, and sent their *wakils* to him to demand their pay. The *wazir* directed Najib Khan to inquire into the matter, and he set his son Zabita Khan, to the work. . . .

[1] *The word "sin" seems to have a wider meaning than that suggested in page elsewhere. There were various "daghs." In the "Chahar Gulzar," the "shamsher" (sword) "dagh" is mentioned.]*

The soldiers, dissatisfied with their *wakils*, and ready for a disturbance, sent thirty or forty of their most violent leaders to get redress for their grievances. These men, complaining and railing against their officers, went to the pavilion of the *wazir*, and, collecting therein a mob, raised a great tumult. The *wazir* heard this, and, proud of his rank and power, came fearlessly out to quell the disturbance. The rioters seized him, and began to abuse him in terms unmentionable. Numbers gathered together from every side, and the mob increased. They tore off his clothes, and in the struggle his turban even fell from his head. Then they dragged him through the streets of Panipat to their camp. The *wazir's* forces, hearing of the disturbance, gathered and prepared to fight; but when they saw their master in the hands of the mutineers, they were helpless. The chiefs of the *dagh* went to the *wazir* with apologies, and brought him a turban and such garments as they could get. The *wazir*, seeing how frightened they were, flew into a rage, and reviled them. Meanwhile a message was brought from the Emperor to the officers, offering to make himself responsible for their pay if they would deliver over the *wazir* to him a prisoner, and telling them that if he escaped from their hands, they would have hard work to get their pay from him.

The passions of the mob being somewhat quieted, their chiefs thought that the best way of saving themselves was to communicate the Emperor's message to the *wazir*. They came humbly before him, with importunities, and brought an elephant, on which they seated him. Hasan Khan, one of the chiefs, took his seat in the *howda* with him, and attended him as his servant to the door of his tent. As soon as the *wazir* had alighted, Hasan Khan also dismounted from the elephant, and mounting a horse went off to the camp. The *wazir* entered his tent, and sat down. He then inquired what had become of Hasan Khan, and on being told, he went out and mounted an elephant. His own officers and soldiers were collected there, prepared to act, and waited only for directions. He gave them orders to kill every man of that riotous party, whoever he might be, and wherever they might find him; not one was to be allowed to escape with life. The Rohillas of Najib Khan and other adherents fell upon the doomed band, and in a short space of time no trace of them was left. Many were killed, and a few with (only) a nose and two ears escaped by flight. 'Imadu-l Mulk was much hurt and troubled by the part the Emperor had taken. In a few days they returned to Dehli, and he, leaving the Emperor under the watch of his confidants, proceeded to Lahore.]

'Imadu-l Mulk Ghaziu-d din seizes the widow of Mu'inu-l Mulk

['Imadul Mulk formed the design of recovering Lahore, and marched for that purpose from Dehli with a large army, taking with him Prince 'Ali Gauhar. They went forward as if on a hunting excursion. Under the advice of Adina Beg Khan, he sent forward from Ludhiyana a force under the command of Saiyid Jamilu-d din Khan, which accomplished the march of forty or fifty *kos* in one day and night, and reached Lahore early on the following morning. The widow of Mu'inu-l Mulk was asleep in her dwelling, and awoke to find herself a prisoner. She was carried to the camp of 'Imadu-l Mulk, who, upon her arrival, waited upon her, and begged to be excused for what he had done. Having consoled her, he kept her near himself, and gave the province of Lahore to Adina Beg Khan for a tribute of thirty *lacs* of rupees. Prince 'Ali Gauhar was annoyed by the complaints and reproaches of the widow of Mu'inu-l Mulk, and tried to induce 'Imadu-l Mulk to reinstate her; but the minister paid no heed to his remonstrances, and annoyed him in every way. The widow, hurt by the treatment she had received, let loose her tongue, and in a loud voice reviled and abused the *wazir*. She added, "This conduct of yours will bring distress upon the realm, destruction to Shah-Jahanabad, and disgrace to the nobles and the State. Ahmad Shah Durrani will soon avenge this disgraceful act and punish you."

Ahmad Shah (Abdali), on hearing of this daring act of 'Imadu-l Mulk, came hastily to Lahore. Adina Beg Khan, being unable to resist, fled towards Hansi and Hissar. 'Imadu-l Mulk was frightened, and by the good offices of Prince 'Ali Gauhar, he succeeded in effecting a reconciliation with the widow of Mu'inu-l Mulk. When Ahmad Shah drew near to Dehli, 'Imadu-l Mulk had no resource but submission, so he sought pardon of his offence through the mediation of the widow. With all the marks of contrition he went forth to meet the Shah, and the widow interceding for him, he was confirmed in his rank and office, upon condition of paying a heavy tribute. On the 7th of Jumada-l awwal, 1170 A.H. (28 Jan. 1757 A.D.), he entered the fortress of Shah-Jahanabad, and had an interview with the Emperor 'Alamgir. He remained in the city nearly a month, plundering the inhabitants, and very few people escaped being pillaged. . . .

When Ahmad Shah demanded the tribute from 'Imadu-l Mulk, the later asked how it could be thought possible for him to have such a sum of money; but he added that if a force of Durranis and a Prince of the house of Timur were sent with him, he might raise a large sum from the country of Sirhind. The Abdali named Prince 'Ali Gauhar, but that Prince had been greatly pained and disgusted by the wilfulness and want of respect shown by 'Imadu-l Mulk on their march to Lahore, so he declined. . . . 'Imadu-l Mulk, having assembled a large force, went into Oudh, and Nawab Shuja'u-d daula marched boldly out of Lucknow to oppose him, and took post at Sandi. Conflicts between their advanced forces went on for several days, but an agreement was arrived at through the medium of

Sa'du-llah Khan, by which Shuja'u-d daula agreed to pay five *lacs* of rupees in cash to furnish supplies.]

Transactions of the year 1173 A.H. (1759-60 A.D.).
Martyrdom of 'Alamgir II[2]

[1]Imadu-l Mulk (Ghaziu-d din Khan), who was very apprehensive of Najibu-d daula, excited Datta Sindhia and Jhanku Mahratta to hostilities against him, and promised them several *lacs* of rupees, on condition of their expelling him from the country which he occupied. The Mahratta chiefs accordingly, at the head of their southern armies, attacked Najibu-d daula with impetuosity, and he, as long as he was able, maintained his ground against that force, which was as numerous as ants or locusts, till at last, being able to hold out no longer, he took refuge in the fort of Sakartal. The southrons laid siege to the fort, and having stopped the supplies of grain, put him to great distress. Sindhia, seeing Najibu-d daula reduced to extremities, sent for 'Imadu-l Mulk from Shah-Jahanabad, in order to complete the measures for chastising him.

'Imadu-l Mulk, suspicious of the Emperor, and knowing that 'Intizamu-d daula Khan-khanan was his chief adviser, murdered that noble in the very act of saying his prayers. He then treacherously sent Mahdi Ali Khan, of Kashmir, to the Emperor, to report that a most saintly *darwesh* from Kandahar had arrived in the city, who was lodged in the *kotila* of Firoz Shah, and that he was well worth seeing. The Emperor, who was very fond of visiting *fakirs*, and particularly such a one as had come from the country of Ahmad Shah, became extremely desirous of seeing him, and went to him almost unattended. When he reached the appointed place,

---

[2][*Sir H. M. Elliot selected this passage from the Akhbaru-l Muhabbat; but as it was copied verbatim from this work, it has been restored to the rightful owner.*]

he stopped at the door of the chamber where his assassins were concealed, and Mahdi 'Ali Khan, relieved him of the sword which he had in his hand, and put it by. As he entered the house, the curtains were down and fastened to the ground. Mirza Babar, son of I'zzu-d din, son-in-law of the Emperor, beginning to suspect foul play, drew his sword, and wounded several of the conspirators. Upon this the myrmidons of 'Imadu-l Mulk surrounded and took him prisoner; and having taken the sword from him, placed him in a *palankin*, and sent him back to the royal prison. Some evil-minded Mughals were expecting the Emperor in the chamber, and when they found him there unattended and alone, they jumped up, and inflicting on him repeated wounds with their daggers, brought him to the ground, and then threw his body out of the window, stripped off all the clothes, and left the corpse naked. After lying on the ground for eighteen hours, his body was taken up by order of Mahdi 'Ali Khan, and buried in the sepulchre of the Emperor Humayun.[3] This tragedy occurred on Thursday, the 20th of Rabi'u-s sani, 1173 A.H. (30th November 1759 A.D.). On the same day a youth named Muhiu-l Millat, son of Muhiu-s Sunnat, son of Kam Bakhsh, was raised to the throne with the title of Shah Jahan III.

'Imadu-l Mulk hastened to Sakartal, and came to an understanding with Najibu-d daula. In the mean time, the report of Ahmad Shah Durrani's invasion spread among the people. 'Imadu-l Mulk, in fear of his life,

---

[3] *The circumstances of this Emperor's death are not mentioned by the ordinary authorities. Dow is the most circumstantial. Compare Mill's British India, vol. ii. p. 473; Grant Duff's History of the Mahrattas, vol. ii. p. 187; Seir Mutaqherin, vol. ii. p. 166; Life of Hafiz Rahmat Khan, p. 57; Elphinstone's India, vol. ii. p. 635; Scott's History of the Deccan, vol. ii. p. 236; Dow's History of India, vol. ii. p. 473; Franklin's Shah Aulum, p. 13.*

saw no other means of safety than in seeking the protection of Suraj Mal, and accordingly departed without delay for that chief's territory. Please God, an account of the arrival of Shah Durrani shall be related hereafter.

Insult to Shah 'Alam

It is a custom among the Hindus that at the *holi* festival they throw dust upon each other, and indulge in practical jokes. On the 14th of Jumada-l awwal, in the twenty-eighth year of the reign of His Majesty Shah 'Alam, when this festival occurred, Anand Rao Narsi dressed up a person in fine garments to represent the Emperor, and applied long false mustaches and a beard to his lips and chin. The person was placed on an old bedstead, with a lad in his arms, in the dress of a woman, to represent the Emperor's daughter, whom he very tenderly loved, and always kept in his presence when he went out in a litter or on an elephant. The bedstead was carried on the shoulders of four men, and before it went several persons of low caste in the habit of the Emperor's attendants, with clubs, umbrellas, and other *insignia* of royalty in their hands. In this manner they proceeded in regular procession, beating drums, and surrounded by a multitude of spectators. They passed by the Jahannuma palace, where the Emperor was sitting. This great insolence, however, excited no indignation in His Majesty's noble mind; but, on the contrary, he ordered a reward of five hundred rupees to be given to those persons. Shah Nizamu-d din, who was an enemy of Anand Rao, availed himself of the opportunity, and having succeeded in kindling the Emperor's anger, represented the matter on His Majesty's part to Maharaja Sindhia, in whose camp Anand Rao resided.... The Maharaja was highly incensed on being informed of this disrespectful and impudent proceeding, and immediately ordered that the tents of Anand Rao should be plundered, and that he should be sent to Raj Muhammad, *dàrogha* of artillery. No sooner was the order passed than his tents and all his property were given up to plunder, and he himself was seized and placed in front of a gun. The Emperor, on being informed of the orders which the Maharaja had given, sent one of his eunuchs to tell the Maharaja that His Majesty was pleased to pardon the offender; but that he hoped, as a warning to others, the Maharaja would turn him out of his camp. Orders were accordingly given by the Maharaja. he was called back from the gun, and his life was spared; but he was disgraced and banished from the presence. Anand Rao remained concealed in the camp for a few days, and after having collected his property which was left from the spoil, he went away to Ujjain.

THIRTIETH YEAR OF THE REIGN, 1202 A.H. (1787-8 A.D.)

Atrocities of Ghulam Kadir

[When Ghulam Kadir Khan and Isma'il Beg Khan had made their way into Dehli by the contrivance of Nazir Mansur 'Ali Khan and the connivance of the Mughal chiefs, Ghulam Kadir assumed the chief authority. He began to oppress the citizens, and demanded money from the Emperor. These proceedings made the Emperor very angry. Ghulam Kadir went to the Emperor to ask him for the pay of the soldiers, and for some supplies to maintain his own dignity. The Emperor replied that if he possessed any money, he would not withhold it. Ghulam Kadir replied that one of the Princes must be placed in his charge, so that he might go and fight with the Mahrattas. The Emperor told him to go out of the city to hunt, and that Sulaiman Shukoh should then be sent to him. He accordingly departed, and fixed his head-quarters near the *kotila* of Firoz Shah. Afterwards the Prince was mounted on an elephant and was brought with his retinue to the camp. The officers presented their *nazars*, and five hundred horse, a regiment of foot and four guns were placed at the door of the Prince's tent as a guard. . . .

6.

Ghulam Kadir proceeded to the palace, ... and urged the Emperor to procure money from somewhere and to give it to him for the pay of the troops. At this juncture a message was brought to Ghulam Kadir from the *Malika Zamaniya* (the queen dowager), offering to give him ten *lacs* of rupees, on condition of Shah 'Alam being deposed, of Prince Bedar Bakht, son of the late Emperor Ahmad Shah, being raised to the throne, and the fort and city being placed in his possession. Ghulam Kadir agreed to his, and confirmed the plan by his word and covenant, expressing his devotion to the house of Babar. On the 26th Shawwal, 1202 A.H. (31st July, 1788 A.D.), he went to the palace, attended by five hundred men, to demand money for the soldiers, and to express his fears of the Emperor. On the Emperor inquiring what he meant, he replied that his enemies and detractors had raised suspicions against him in the Emperor's mind, and to guard against this he required that the charge of the palace should be placed in the hands of his own people, so that he might come and state freely what he had to represent. The Emperor replied that he seemed destined to be the ruin of the royal house, and that his name would stand infamous on the page of history. Nazir Mansur 'Ali Khan observed that Isma'il Khan was present with a statement and agreement, and that (for confirming it by oath) he had also brought the Holy Kuran. He was called forward, the compact was confirmed upon the Holy Kuran, under the signatures of himself and Ghulam Kadir. The Emperor said, "I place myself under the protection of the Kuran, and submit to your wishes."

Having obtained the Emperor's consent, the *Nazir* placed the gates of the palace in charge of Ghulam Kadir's men.... Four thousand horse were posted in and about the palace, ..., and all the environs were in the possession of the men of Ghulam Kadir and the *Mirza* (Bedar Bakht). They took possession of the doors of the female apartments, beat the eunuchs with stones and sticks, seized upon the goods and furniture, and took the wardrobe and the store-rooms out of the hands of the royal servants. A few personal attendants and eunuchs were all that remained with the Emperor. No one was left who could go out to ascertain what was passing, and the Emperor was in great trouble and anxiety. At that moment Prince Akbar said, "One choice is yet left: if you will allow us, we brothers will all fall upon those traitors, and will bravely encounter martyrdom." He replied, "No one can escape the decrees of the Almighty, there is no contending against doom; the power is now in the hands of others." Prince Akbar raised a great cry, drew his sword, and placed it to his throat to kill himself. The Emperor snatched the sword from his hand, and put it to his own throat. A cry arose from all who were present, and the noise spread through the palace. Ghulam Kadir came in alarmed. The Emperor, with great politeness, called him near, and placing his head upon his own breast, said in his ear, "Twenty *lacs* of rupees have been provided, but let them be expended in the business of the Mahrattas, and not in a way that will bring censure and lasting disgrace upon me." ....

On the 27th Shawwal Ghulam Kadir, having come to an understanding with Isma'il Beg Khan, went into the presence of the Emperor, who was seated in his private apartments, and began to speak fawningly. The Emperor said, "I relied upon your promise and your oath on the Kurán, and kept myself in private, tell me what you require, for I have no remedy." Ghulam Kadir frowned, and replied, "I have no reliance on you. He who speaks of sitting in private should give up the claim to sovereignty." At that moment Gul Muhammad Khan brought forward Prince Bedar Bakht. Ghulam Kadir insolently stepped forward, and took the Emperor's dagger from his girdle, while his companions wrested the swords from the hands of the Princes. The Emperor's personal attendants and the eighteen Princes were removed

ed to the *salatin*.⁴ Ghulam Kadir then took the hand of Prince Bedar Bakht, and placed him on the royal seat. The chiefs who were present made their offerings, and the drums were beaten to proclaim the name of Bedar Bakht. He thus ascended the throne on the 27th Shawwal, 1204 A.H. (22nd June, 1790).

On the 8th Zi-l ka'da Ghulam Kadir sent his stern officers to Bedar Bakht for ten *lacs* of rupees. He excused himself, saying that the Imperial family had been swept clean, but he would send what he could scrape together. He sent some vessels of silver and other articles, and said that if more was required, application should be made to Sindhia and the Rajas who were well affected towards the Imperial throne. Rohilla 'Ali said, "Your Majesty must go into the private apartments, for the money will not be obtained without some trouble." He said, "If there is any more money, you are welcome to it. I came out of the *salatin* with a shirt and an old pair of trowsers, which I still have; but you know all about it." Ghulam Kadir took the gold and silver-mounted articles from the apartments of Shah 'Alam and the princes and princesses, then piled them in a heap and burnt them, and sent the metal to the mint to be coined. He took several cart-loads of swords, daggers, and buskets, belonging to the Emperor and Princes; some he gave to his companions, and some he sent to the store-house.

Shah 'Alam and the Princes were kept as prisoners in the Moti Mahall. Ghulam Kadir ordered that Prince Akbar and Prince Sulaiman Shukoh should be bound and whipped by the carpet-spreaders. Shah 'Alam exclaimed, "Whatever is to be done, do to me! These are young and innocent." Bedar Bakht now came in. Ghulam Kadir abused them, and put every one of them

⁴ [*This word recurs, and, as here used, it probably is an abbreviation of the words* deorhi salatin, *apartments of the Princes.*

in the hot sunshine. Bedar Bakht, having sat there a little while, informed him how to find money, and said, "My servants are at your command, threaten them, and ask for it." The female attendants of the palace were then bound, and hot oil being poured on the palms of their hands and their feet, they gave information of two ice vaults from which a box of gold, silver and mounted vessels was taken. . . . Shah 'Alam was sitting in the sun and complaining, when Ghulam Kadir said to some truculent Afghans, "Throw this babbler down and blind him." Those men threw him down, and passed the needle into his eyes. They kept him down safe on the ground for a time with blows of sticks, and Ghulam Kadir asked him derisively if he saw anything, and he replied, "Nothing but the Holy Kuran between me and you." All night long he and his children and the women of his palace kept up loud cries. Ghulam Kadir remained that night in the Moti Mahall, and hearing these cries, he writhed like a snake, and directed his servants to beat and kill those who made them. But some of these men dreaded the questioning of the day of judgment, and held their hands.

On the 9th Zi-l ka'da, . . . Ghulam Kadir said to Bedar Bakht, "Come out, and I will show you a sight." Perforce, he went out of the door, and sat down. Ghulam Kadir went to Shah 'Alam, and said, "Find me some gold, or I will send you to join the dead." Shah 'Alam reviled and reproached him, saying, "I am in your power, cut off my head, for it is better to die than to live like this." Ghulam Kadir sprang up, and threw himself upon the Emperor's bosom. Kandahari Khan and Purdil Khan seized his hands, two of their companions held his feet, Kandahari Khan tore out one of his eyes, and that bloodthirsty reckless ruffian tore out the other with his own hands, amid the wailings of the Emperor. Ghulam Kadir then gave orders that the needle should be pased into the eyes of Prince Akbar, Sulaiman Shukoh, and Ahsan Bakht. The ladies came from behind their curtains, and threw themselves at the feet of Ghulam Kadir, to pray for mercy; but he kicked them on their breasts, and sent them away. The heart of Miyar[a] Singh was in flames, and, overpowered with rage, he cried. "Ghulam Kadir! cease your fury, and withdraw your hands from these helpless (princes); for if you do not, you will hardly escape from me." Seeing his passion, Ghulam Kadir arose, and said, "Pinion all three of them, and I will consider what to do with them another time." He then ordered some of his followers who were present to beat them with sticks till they were senseless, and to put them in prison. Then he called for a painter, and said, "Paint my likeness at once, sitting, knife in hand, upon the breast of Shah 'Alam, digging out his eyes." He then forbad his attendants to bring any food or water either to Shah 'Alam or his sons.

The poor Emperor kept groaning and crying, but no one heeded him. Next day Bedar Bakht sent two surgeons to dress his wounds, and ordered him to be supplied with water. His servants reported to him that the poor Emperor's eyes were running with blood, and that the (only) water he had to drink was what flowed from his eyes. . . . Ghulam Kadir went to Shah 'Alam, and seizing him by the beard, said, "I have inflicted all this severity upon you for your faults, but I spare your life for God's sake, otherwise I should have no scruple in tearing you limb from limb." On the 12th Zi-l ka'da he went into the jewel-house, and took out a chest and a box of jewels; he also took several copies of the *Kuran*, and eight large baskets of books out of the library. On the 13th his spies informed him that two sisters of Sulaiman Shukoh, one aged five years and the other four, had died from thirst. When he heard it, he laughed and said, "Let them be buried where they lie." One of his men went to Bedar Bakht, and said, "Ghulam Kadir

[a] [*A very doubtful name. It is variously written "Matar," "Biyar," etc.*]

wants the jewels you have." The Prince immediately brought them out of his private apartments, and handed them over.

Next day Ghulam Kadir, taking Bedar Bakht with him, went to Malika Zamaniya and Sahiba Mahall,[a] and said, "Where is the money that was promised?" They said, "What you demand from us is a mere fancy and dream of yours." When he heard this, he sent a person into the private apartments, with directions to bring them both out, with only the garments they stood upright in, and to seize upon all the money and valuables which could be found. Accordingly they took Malika Zamaniya and Sahiba Mahall in the dresses they were wearing (*ba libas-i badan*), and placing them in a *rath*, conducted them with three hundred attendants to the Moti Mahall. Workmen were then sent in to break down the roof and walls. Neither Nadir Shah, Ahmad Shah Durrani, nor Taraji Bhao, had ever dreamed of plundering the ladies of the *harem*; but now all the valuables, the accumulations of fifty or sixty years, were brought out. . . .

On the 25th Zi-l ka'da Ghulam Kadir called Prince Akbar, Sulaiman Shukoh, and the other Princes, nineteen in number, before him, and with harsh words called upon them to sing and dance before him. They declined; but he would not listen to them, saying that he had long heard praises of their singing and dancing. He then commanded his attendants to cut off the Princes' noses if they did not sing. The Princes and boys, seeing there was no escaping from his commands, did as they were directed, and sang and danced. He was very pleased, and asked them what recompense they desired. They said, "Our father and children are in great want of water and food, we ask for some." He gave his consent. He then turned all his attendants out of the room, and, placing his head upon the knees of Prince Akbar,

[a] [*Both these ladies were widows of Muhammad Shah. The former was a daughter of the Emperor Farrukh Siyar.*]

went to sleep, leaving his sword and knife in their presence. He closed his eyes for an hour (*sa'at*), and then getting up, he slapped each of them on the neck, and said, "Can such (craven) spirits entertain the idea of reigning.? I wanted to try your courage. If you had any spirit, you would have made an end of me with my sword and dagger." Then abusing them in foul disgusting words, he sent them out of his presence.

Afterwards he called for Bedar . Bakht and his brothers, and placed wine before them. With his own hands he several times filled the cups, and they continued drinking till evening, when they got up and danced and sang, and acted disgracefully. A eunuch came in, and told him that a daughter of Shah 'Alam, a child of ten years old, had died of hunger and thirst crouching on the earth. He cried, "Bury her just as she is, in the place where she lies." When Raja Miyar Singh heard of these things, he sent bread and provisions for Shah 'Alam and his children. Ghulam Kadir was angry—he sent for the Raja, and frowning at him, asked, "What concern have you with those men? Remove your people from the watch, for I will place Rohillas to keep guard." The Raja told him that the day of retribution for these deeds was approaching, and that it was not well to offened the chiefs. He replied that he would do whatever came into his heart. . . .

On the 17th Zi-l ka'da (*sic*) Wai Khaili (his myrmidon) reported to him that he had probed the walls of the apartments of Malika Zamaniya and Sahiba Mahall till he had made them like sieves, that he had stripped everybody, and that no hole had been left unsearched by his fingers. He had found a few pearls. One of Bedar Bakht's ladies had died of fright at what was passing, and now the Afghans, having stripped the ladies, were thinking about taking them with (without?) gowns or bodices.¹ He added, "The power is in your

---

¹ *ba jama u kurta.*

hands, but it is not well to cast such shame upon the honour of princes." It all depended on his pleasure, but Ghulam Kadir replied that when the Emperor's servants plundered his father's private apartments, they had done worse than that to his women.⁸ "Now," said he, "it shall be a sight for the time, for my men shall take the hands of kings' daughters, conduct them home, and take possession of their persons without marriage." He then ordered Wai Khaili to go and take possession of the house of Khairu-n nisa Begam, sister of Shah 'Alam, to strip her daughters and women naked, and to search for jewels. After taking . . . all they could find, he asked the Princes for gold, and they replied, "You have taken all we have, and we are now ready to die." At his command the stony-hearted carpet-spreaders beat them so that the blood gushed from their mouths and noses. Then they placed the Princes in the *salatin*.

Ghulam Kadir heard from Wai Khaili of the beauty of the daughters of Mirza Haika and Mirza Jaika (?), and when he was sitting in the Moti Mahall in the evening, he ordered these unhappy ladies to be placed before him without veils or curtains. He was pleased with their beauty, showed them to his boon companions, and acted indecently to every one of them. When Bedar Bakht was informed of this, he beat himself upon the head and bosom, and sent an attendant to the ruffian, to dissuade him from such actions. He replied (sarcastically), "What power has this slave to do anything against His Majesty?" He (Bedar Bakht) then wrote to Raja Miyar Singh, who shuddered when he read the letter, and went to Ghulam Kadir. The Raja called Ghulam Kadir out of the private room, and said to him, "It is not right to deal thus

⁸["On this occasion the Emperor is said by tradition to have transmuted Ghulam Kadir Khan into a *haram* page."—*Keene's Fall of the Mughal Empire*, pp. 101, 200. There is no mention of this in the 'Ibratnama, and the narrative is rather against the tradition.]

with the daughters of enemies. No one seizes sons and daughters for the faults of their fathers. Shah 'Alam did not cast any evil looks upon the daughters or sisters of your father; refrain from such proceedings." Ghulam Kadir answered (*in coarse terms to the effect*) that he intended to take them into his *harem* and make them his concubines, and as for the other Princesses, he would give them to his Afghans, so that they might have a chance of bringing forth men of courage. Raja Miyar Singh, against the will of Ghulam Kadir, went into the room, cast a sheet over (the Princesses' heads), and sent them home.]

Death of Ghulam Kadir

[It is said that on the 18th Rabi'u-l awwal, Ghulam Kadir (*after being defeated by the forces of Sindhia*), started off for Ghaus-kada, his home, with only a few trusted followers, mounted on swift horses. In the darkness of the night his companions lost him; he went one way, and they went another. He endeavoured to find them, but did not succeed. The road was full of water and mud, and the horse putting his foot into a hole, rolled Ghulam Kadir to the ground. The night was dark, and the way bristled with thorny acacias, so that he knew not which way to turn. When the morning came, he looked around, and seeing some inhabited place, he proceeded thither. On reaching the habitation, he put his head into the house of a *brahman*. The master of the house, seeing a stranger in such a state, asked him what was the matter. Ghulam Kadir answered that . . .* But his own action betrayed him. He took off a diamond ring from his finger, and gave it to the housekeeper as an inducement to guard him all day, and to guide him at night towards Ghaus-kada. The *brahman* knew of his infamous character and evil deeds. The *brahman* himself, in days gone by, had suffered at the hands of

*[*The words of the answer are not complete.*]

the ruffian, and his village had been ravaged. His oppressor was now in his power, and he made the door fast. . . .

The *brahman* went in search of some chief who would appreciate the information he had to give, and was led by fortune to the tents of 'Ali Bahadur, to whom he communicated his intelligence. 'Ali Bahadur showed him great attention, and sent a large party of horse forward with him, while he himself followed. . . . The horsemen entered the *brahman's* house, seized their prisoner, and bound him. With various indignities they brought him to 'Ali Bahadur, . . . who sent him to the fort of the Mahrattas, . . . under charge of Rana Khan, who put a chain upon his legs, a collar on his neck, and conveyed him in a bullock-carriage to Sindhia, guarded by two regiments of sepoys and a thousand horse. . . . On the 4th Jumada-s sani, under the orders of Sindhia, the ears of Ghulam Kadir were cut off and hung round his neck, his face was blackened, and he was carried round the camp and city. Next day his nose and upper lip were cut off, and he was again paraded. On the third day he was thrown upon the ground, his eyes were torn out, and he was once more carried round. After that his hands were cut off, then his feet, and last of all his head. The corpse was then hung neck downwards from a tree. A trustworthy person relates that a black dog, white round the eyes, came and sat under the tree and licked up the blood as it dripped. The spectators threw stones and clods at it, but still it kept there. On the third day, the corpse disappeared and the dog also vanished. Maharaja Sindhia sent the ears and eye-balls to the Emperor Shah 'Alam.]

CHAHAR GULSHAN
OF
RAM CHATAR MAN

This work, which is also called *Akhbaru-l Nawadir*, "Accounts of Rare Things," was composed by Rai Chatar Man Kayath in the year 1173 A.H. (1759 A.D.), the last sheets being finished only a week before his death. As it was left in an unconnected shape, it was arranged and edited, after his death, by his grandson, Rai Bhan Raizada, in 1204 A.H. (1789-90 A.D.), as is shown by a chronogram in the Preface; but as the work ends with the accession of the nominal Emperor Shah Jahan the Second in A.H. 1173, it is evident that the Editor has added nothing to his grandfather's labours.

The Editor states that when Chatar Man had travelled the road of eternity, he, as a dutiful grandson, was anxious to display this nosegay of wisdom to some effect, in order that those who wander in the garden of eloquence might, by a close inspection of its beauties, which are endowed with perpetual verdure, feel the bud of their heart expand with delight.

The *Chahar Gulshan* or "Four Gardens," is, as the name implies, divided into four Books, and is said by the Editor to contain so much information in a small compass that it resembles the ocean placed in a cup. The historical part is a mere abstract, and of no value, nor are any authorities quoted for its statements; but the work has other points of interest, especially in the matter of the Biographies of the Muhammadan saints, which are written in a true spirit of belief, though the writer is a Hindu. The accounts of the Hindu fakirs, the Itineraries, and the Statistical Tables of the twenty-two *subas* of Hindustan, are also useful, though it is to be regretted that the latter are not given in sufficient detail to enable us to institute safe comparisons between its results and those given in the *Ain-i Akbari*.

CONTENTS

Book I. The Kings of Hindustan from Judhishthira to the fall of the Mughal empire, with a statistical account of the several *subas* of Hindustan proper, and of their Rulers and Saints, p. 4.—II. An account of the southern *subas* of India, and of their Rulers and Saints, p. 147.—III. Itineraries from Dehli to the different quarters of India. p. 219.—IV. An account of the Hindu *fakirs*, p. 282.

The *Chahar Gulshan* is common in India, and I have seen several copies, none conspicuously good, except that in the possession of Nawab 'Ali Muhammad Khan of Jhajjar.

SIZE—Quarto, 560 pages of 13 lines each.

TARIKH-I IBRAHIM KHAN

[According to the author's statement in his Preface, "These wonderful events, forming a volume of warning for men of sagacity, are chronicled by the hasty pen of the humblest of slaves, 'Ali Ibrahim Khan, during the administration of the illustrious noble of celestial grandeur, the centre of the circle of prosperity, the ally of foe-crushing victory, the sun of the firmament of wisdom, the unfurler of the standards of pomp and dignity, the excellent prince bearing the highest titles, the chief of mighty and magnificent rulers,—the Governor General, Charles, Earl of Cornwallis, may his good fortune last for ever!"

At the end of the volume we are informed that "this book, composed by the illustrious Nawab Ibrahim Khan Bahadur, was completely written from beginning to end by the pen of Mulla Bakhsh at the town of Benares, and was finished in 1201 A.H. (1786 A.D.).

This work is very valuable for the clear and succinct account it gives of the Mahrattas. The whole of it was translated for Sir H. M. Elliot by the late Major Fuller, and is here printed with the exception of some unimportant passages, and the account of the battle of Panipat, which has been previously drawn from another work written by one who took part in the battle.

Size—6 inches by 4; 219 pages of 9 lines each.]

EXTRACTS

As the comprehension of the design of this work is dependent on a previous acquaintance with the origin and genealogy of Balaji Rao, the eloqutnt pen will first proceed to the discussion of that subject.

Origin and Genealogy of the Mahrattas

Be it not hidden, that in the language of the people of the Dakhin, these territories and their dependencies are called "Dihast,"[1] and the inhabitants of the region are styled "Mahrattas." The Mahratti dialect is adopted exclusively by these classes, and the chieftainship of the Mahrattas is centred in the Bhonsla tribe. The lineage of the Bhonslas is derived from the Udipur Rajas, who bear the title of Rana; and the first of these, according to popular tradition, was one of the descendants of Naushirwan. At the time when the holy warriors of the army of Islam subverted the realms of Iran, Naushirwan's descendants were scattered in every direction; and one of them, having repaired to Hindustan, was promoted to the dignity of a Raja. In a word, one of the Rana's progeny afterwards quitted the territory of Udipur, in consequence of the menacing and disordered aspect of his affairs, and having proceeded to the country of the Dakhin, fixed his abode in the Carnatic. The chiefs of the Dakhin, regarding the majesty of his family with respect and reverence, entered into the most amicable relations with him. His descendants separated into two families; one the Aholias, the other the Bhonslas.

Memoir of Sahuji, of the tribe of Bhonslas

Sahuji was first inrolled among the number of Nizam Shah's retainers, but afterwards entered into the service

[1][Properly "deshasth." See Grant Duff, vol. i. p. 11.]

of Ibrahim 'Adil Shah, who was the ruler of the Kokan. In return for the faithful discharge of his duties, he received in *jagir* the *parganas* of Poona, etc., where he made a permanent settlement after the manner of the *zamindars*. Towards the close of his life, having attained the high honour of serving the Emperor Jahangir, he was constantly in attendance on him, while his son Sivaji stayed at the *jagir*. As Ibrahim 'Adil Shah for the space of two years was threatened with impending death, great disorder and confusion prevailed in his territories from the long duration of his illness; and the troops and retainers, whom he had stationed here and there, for the purpose of garrisoning the forts, and protecting the frontier of the Kokan, abandoned themselves to neglect in consequence of their master's indisposition.

Memoir of Siva, the son of Sahu

.... Ultimately, the Emperor Aurangzeb, the bulwark of religion, resolved upon proceeding to the Dakhin, and in the year 1093 A.H. bestowed fresh lustre on the city of Aurangabad by the favour of his august presence. For a period of twenty-five years he strove to subvert the Mahratta rule; but as several valiant chieftains displayed the utmost zeal and activity in upholding their dynasty, their extermination could not be satisfactorily accomplished. Towards the close of His Majesty's lifetime, a truce was concluded with the Mahrattas, on these terms, viz. that three per cent, out of the revenues drawn from the Imperial dominions in the Dakhin should be allotted to them by way of *sar deshmukhi;* and accordingly Ahsan Khan, commonly called Mir Malik, set out from the threshold of royalty with the documents confirming this grant to the Mahrattas; in order that, after the treaty had been duly ratified, he might bring the chiefs of that tribe to the court of the monarch of the world. However, before he had time to deliver these documents into their custody, a royal mandate was issued, directing him to return and bring back the papers in question with him. About this time, His Majesty Aurangzeb 'Alamgir hastened to the eternal gardens of Paradise, at which period his successor Shah 'Alam (Bahadur Shah) was gracing the Dakhin with his presence. The latter settled ten per cent out of the produce belonging to the peasantry as *sar deshmukhi* on the Mahrattas, and furnished them with the necessary documents confirming the grant.[2]

When Shah 'Alam (Bahadur Shah) returned from the Dakhin to the metropolis, Daud Khan remained behind to officiate for *Amiru-l umara* Zulfikar Khan in the government of the provinces. He cultivated a good understanding with the Mahrattas, and concluded an amicable treaty on the following footing, viz. that in addition to the above-mentioned grant of a tithe as *sar deshmukhi*, a fourth of whatever amount was collected in the country should be their property, while the other three-fourths should be paid into the royal exchequer. This system of division was accordingly put in practice; but no regular deed granting the fourth share, which in the dialect of the Dakhin is called *chauth*, was delivered to the Mahrattas. When Muhammad Farrukh Siyar sat as Emperor on the throne of Dehli, he entertained the worst suspicions against *Amiru-l umara* Saiyid Husain 'Ali Khan, the chief of the Barha Saiyids. He dismissed him to a distance from his presence by appointing him to the control of the province of the Dakhin. On reaching his destination, the latter applied himself rigorously to the task of organizing the affairs of that kingdom; but royal letters were incessantly despatched to the address of the chief of the Mahrattas, and more especially to Raja Sahu, urging him to persist in hostilities with *Amiru-l umara*. . . .

In the year 1129 A.H. (1717 A.D.), by the intervention of Muhammad Anwar Khan Burhanpuri and Sankaraji Malhar, he concluded a peace with the Mahrattas,[3] on

[2] *See Vol VII. p. 408 (Original Edition.)*
[3] *See Vol. VII. p. 466 (Or. Ed.)*

condition that they would refrain from committing depredations and robberies, and would always maintain 18,000 horsemen out of their tribe wholly at the service of the *Nazim* of the Dakhin. At the time that this treaty was ratified, he sealed and delivered the documents confirming the grant of the fourth of the revenues, and the *sar deshmukhi* of the province of the Dakhin, as well as proceeds of the Kokan and other territories, which were designated as their ancient dominions. At the same period Raja Sahu appointed Balaji, son of Basu Nath (Biswa Nath), who belonged to the class of Kokani Brahmins, to fill the post of his *vakil* at the Court of the Emperor; and in all the districts of the six provinces of the Dakhin he appointed two revenue commissioners of his own, one to collect the *sar deshmukhi*, and the other to receive the fourth share or *chauth*. . . .

Amiru-l umara Husain 'Ali, having increased the *mansabs* held by Balaji, the son of Basu Nath, and Sankaraji Malhar, deputed them to superintend the affairs of of the Dakhin, and sent them to join 'Alim 'Ali Khan. . . . . After the death of Balaji, the son of Basu Nath, his son, named Baji Rao, became his successor, and Holkar, who was a servant of Balaji Rao, having urged the steed of daring, at his master's instigation, at full speed from the Dakhin towards Malwa, put the (*subadar*) Garidhar Bahadur to death on the field of battle. After this occurrence, the government of that province was conferred on Muhammad Khan Bangash; but owing to the turbulence of the Mahrattas, he was unable to restore it to proper order. On his removal from office, the administration of that region was entrusted to Raja Jai Singh Sawai. Unity of faith and religion strengthened the bonds of amity between Baji Rao and Raja Jai Singh; and this circumstance was a source of additional power and influence to the former, insomuch that during the year 1146 (1733 A.D.) he had the audacity to advance and make an inroad into the confines of Hindustan. The grand wazir *'Itimadu-d daula* Kamru-d din Khan;

7.

was first selected by the Emperor Muhammad Shah to oppose him, and on the second occasion Muzaffar Khan, the brother of Samsamu-d daula Khan-dauran. These two, having entered the province of Malwa, pushed on as far as Sironj, but Baji Rao returned to the Dakhin without hazarding an engagement. . . .

In the second year after the above-mentioned date, Baji Rao attempted another invasion of Hindustan, when the *wazir* 'Itimadu-d daula Kamru-d din Khan Bahadur and the Nawab Khan-dauran Khan went forth from Dehli to give him battle. . . . On this occasion several engagements took place, but victory fell to the lot of the *wazir*; and peace having been ultimately concluded, they both returned to Dehli.

In the third year from the aforesaid date, through the mediation of *Amiru-l umara* Khan-dauran Khan Bahadur, the government of Malwa was bestowed on Baji Rao, whereby his power and influence was increased twofold. The Rao in question, having entered Malwa with a numerous force, soon reduced the province to a satisfactory state of order. About the same time he attacked the Raja of Bhadawar, and after putting him to flight, devasted his territory. From thence he despatched Pilaji with the view of subduing the kingdom of Antarbed (Doab), which is situated between the Ganges and Jumna. At that very time Nawab Burhanu-l Mulk had moved out of his own province, and advanced through Antarbed to the vicinity of Agra. Pilaji therefore crossed the Jumna, and engaged in active hostilities against the above-named Nawab; but having been vanquished in battle, he was forced to take to flight, and rejoin Baji Rao. An immense number of his army were drowned while crossing the Jumna; but as for those who were captured or taken prisoners, the Nawab presented each one with two rupees and a cloth, and gave him permission to depart. Baji Rao, becoming downcast and dispirited after meeting with this ignominious defeat, turned his face from that quarter, and proceeded towards Dehli. . . .

Samsamu-d daula Amiru-l umara Bahadur, after considerable deliberation, sallied forth from Shah-Jahanabad with intent to check the enemy; but Baji Rao, not deeming it expedient at the time to kindle the flame of war, retired towards Agra, and Amiru-l umara, considering himself fortunate enough in having effected so much, re-entered the metropolis. This was the first occasion on which the Mahrattas extended their aggressions so far as to threaten the environs of the metropolis. Though most of the men in the Mahratta army are unendowed with the excellence of noble and illustrious birth, and husbandmen, carpenters, and shopkeepers abound among their soldiery, yet, as they undergo all sorts of toil and fatigue in prosecuting a guerilla warfare, they prove superior to the easy and effeminate troops of Hind, who for the most part are of more honourable birth and calling. If this class were to apply their energies with equal zeal to the profession, and free themselves from the trammels of indolence, their prowess would excel that of their rivals, for the aristocracy ever possess more spirit than the vulgar herd. The free-booters who form the vanguard of the Mahratta forces, and marching in advance of their main body, ravage the enemy's country, are called *puikarahs*[a] the Mahratta troops who are stationed here and there by way of picquets at a distance from the army, for the purpose of keeping a vigilant watch, are styled *mati,* and *chhappah* is synonymous in their dialect with a night-attack. Their food consists chiefly of cakes made of *jawar,* or *bajra, dal, arhad,* with a little butter and red pepper; and hence it is that, owing to the irascibility of their tempers, gentleness is never met with in their dispositions. The ordinary dress worn by these people comprises a turban, tunic, *selāh* (loose mantle), and *janghiah* (short drawers). Among their horses are many mares, and among the offensive weapons used by this tribe there are but few fire-arms, most of

[a] *Pujkarahs* (Persians).

the men being armed with swords, spears, or arrows instead. The system of military service established among them is this: each man, according to his grade, receives a fixed salary in cash and clothes every year. They call their stables *pagah*, and the horsemen who are mounted on chargers belonging to a superior officer are styled *bargirs*. . . .

Balaji's Exploits

When Baji Rao, in the year 1153 A.H. (1740 A.D.), on the banks of the river Nerbadda, bore the burden of his existence to the shores of non-entity, his son, Balaji Rao, became his successor, and after the manner of his father, engaged vigorously in the prosecution of hostilities, the organization and equipment of a large army, and the preparation of all the munitions of war. His son continued to pass his days, sometimes at war, and at other times at peace, with the Nawab Asaf Jah. At length, in the year 1165 (1750 A.D.), Sahu Rao, the successor of Sambhaji, passed away, and the supreme authority departed out of the direct line of the Bhonslas. Balaji Rao selected another individual of that family, in place of Sahu's son, to occupy the post of Raja, and seated him on the throne, whilst he reserved for himself the entire administration of all the affairs of the kingdom. Having then degraded the ancient chieftains from the lofty position they had held, he denuded them of their dignity and influence, and began aggrandizing the Kokani Brahmins, who were of the same caste as himself. He also constituted his cousin, Sadashco Rao, commonly called Bhao Rao, his chief agent and prime minister. The individual in question was of acute understanding, and thoroughly conversant with the proper method of government. Through the influence of his energetic counsels, many undertakings were constantly brought to a successful issue, the recital of which would lead to too great prolixity. In short, besides holding the fortress of Bijapur, he took possession anew of Daulatabad, the seat of government of the illustrious sovereigns, together with districts yielding sixty *lacs* of rupees, after forcibly wresting it out of the hands of Nizamu-l Mulk Nizam 'Ali Khan Bahadur. He likewise took into his service Ibrahim Khan Gardi, who had a well-organized train of European artillery with him.

The Abdali Monarch

Ahmad Shah Abdali, in the year 1171 A.H. (1757-8 A.D.), came from the country of Kandahar to Hindustan, and on the 7th of Jumada-l awwal of that year, had an interview with the Emperor 'Alamgir II., at the palace of Shah-Jahanabad; he exercised all kinds of severity and oppression on the inhabitants of that city, and united the daughter of A'azzu-d din, own brother to His Majesty, in the bonds of wedlock with his own son, Timur Shah. After an interval of a month, he set out to coerce Raja Suraj Mal Jat, who, from a distant period, had extended his sway over the province of Agra, as far as the environs of the city of Dehli. In three days he captured Balamgarh, situated at a distance of fifteen *kos* from Dehli, which was furnished with all the requisites for standing a siege, and was well manned by Suraj Mal's followers. After causing a general massacre of the garrison, he hastened towards Mathura, and having razed that ancient sanctuary of the Hindus to the ground, made all the idolators fall a prey to his relentless sword. Then he returned to Agra, and deputed his Commander-in-Chief, Jahan Khan, to reduce all the forts belonging to the Jat chieftain. At this time a dreadful pestilence broke out with great virulence in the Shah's army, so that he was forced to abandon his intention of chastising Suraj Mal, and unwillingly made up his mind to repair to his own kingdom.

On his return, as soon as he reached Dehli, the Emperor 'Alamgir went forth with Najibu-d daula Bahadur, and had an interview with him on the margin of the Maksudabad lake, when he preferred sore complaints against 'Imadu-l Mulk Ghaziu-d din Khan Bahadur, who was at that time at Farrukhabad, engaged in exciting seditious tumults. The Shah, after forming a matrimonial alliance with the daughter of his late Majesty Muhammad Shah, and investing Najibu-d daula with the title of *Amriu-l umara* and the dignified post of *bakhshi*, set out for Lahore. As soon as he had planted his sublime standard on that spot, he conferred both the government of Lahore and Multan on his son, Timur Shah, and leaving Jahan Khan behind with him, proceeded himself to Kandahar.

Jahan Khan despatched a warrant to Adina Beg Khan, who at that time had taken up his residence at Lakhi Jangal, investing him with the supreme control of the territory of the Doab, along with a *khil'at* of immense value, and adopted the most conciliatory measures towards him, whereupon the latter, esteeming this amicable attention as a mark of good fortune, applied himself zealously to the proper administration of the Doab. When Jahan Khan, however, summoned him to his presence, he did not consider it to his advantage to wait upon him; so, quitting the territory of the Doab, he retired into the hill-country. After this occurrence, Jahan Khan appointed a person named Murad Khan to the charge of the Doab, and sent Sarbuland Khan and Sarfaraz Khan, of the Abdali tribe, along with him to assist him. Adina Beg Khan, having united the Sikh nation to his own forces, advanced to give battle to Murad Khan, when Sarbuland Khan quaffed the cup of martyrdom on the field of action, and Murad Khan and Sarfaraz Khan, seeing no resource left them but flight, returned to Jahan Khan, and the Sikhs ravaged all the districts of the Doab.

As soon as active hostilities were commenced between Najibu-d daula and 'Imadu-l Mulk, the latter set out from Farrukhabad towards Dehli, to oppose the former, and forwarded letters to Balaji Rao and his cousin Bhao, soliciting aid, and inviting the Mahratta army to espouse his cause. Bhao, who was always cherishing plans in his head for the national aggrandizement, counselled Balaji Rao to despatch an army for the conquest of the territories of Hindustan, which he affirmed to be then, as it were, an assembly unworthy of reverence, and a rose devoid of thorns.

Memoir of Raghunath Rao

In 1171 A.H. (1757-8 A.D.) Raghunath Rao, a brother of Balaji Rao, accompanied by Malhar Rao Holkar, Shamsher Bahadur, and Jayaji Sindhia, started from the Dakhin towards Dehli at the head of a gallant and irresistible army, to subdue the dominions of Hindustan. As soon as they reached Agra, they turned off to Shah-Jhanabad in company with 'Imadu-l Mulk, the *wazir*, who was the instigator of the irruption made by this torrent of destruction. After a sanguinary engagement, they ejected Najibu-d daula from the city of Dehli, and consigned the management of the affairs of government to the care of 'Imadu-l Mulk, the *wazir*.

Raghunath Rao and the rest of the Mahratta chiefs set out from Dehli towards Lahore, at the solicitation of Adina Beg Khan, of whom mention has been briefly made above. After leaving the suburbs of Dehli, they arrived first at Sirhind, where they fought an action with 'Abdu-s Samad Khan, who had been installed in the government of that place by the Abdali Shah, and took him prisoner. Turning away from thence, they pushed on to Lahore, and got ready for a conflict with Jahan Khan, who was stationed there. The latter, however, being alarmed at the paucity of his troops in comparison with the multitude of the enemy, resolved at once to seek safety in flight. Accordingly, in the month of Sha'ban, 1171 A.H. (April, 1758 A.D.), he pursued the road to Kabul with the utmost speed, accompanied by Timur Shah, and made a present to the enemy of the heavy baggage and property that he had accumulated during his administration of that region. The Mahratta chieftains followed in pursuit of Timur

Shah as far as the river Attock, and then retraced their steps to Lahore. This time the Mahrattas extended their sway up to Multan. As the rainy season had commenced, they delivered over the province of Lahore to Adina Beg Khan, on his promising to pay a tributary offering of seventy-five *lacs* of rupees; and made up their minds to return to the Dakhin, being anxious to behold again their beloved families at home.

On reaching Dehli in the course of their return, they made straight for their destination, after leaving one of their warlike chieftains, named Janku, at the head of a formidable army in the vicinity of the metropolis. It chanced that in the year 1172 A.H. (1758-9 A.D.) Adina Beg Khan passed away; whereupon Jankuji entrusted the government of the province of Lahore to a Mahratta, called Sama, whom he despatched thither. He also appointed Sadik Beg Khan, one of Adina Beg Khan's followers, to the administration of Sirhind, and gave the management of the Doab to Adina Beg Khan's widow. Sama, after reaching Lahore, applied himself to the task of government, and pushed on his troops as far as the river Attock. In the meanwhile, 'Imadu-l Mulk, the *wazir*, caused Shah 'Alamgir II to suffer martyrdom, in retaliation for an ancient grudge, and placed the son of Muhi'u-s Sunnat, son of Kam Bakhsh, son of Aurangzeb 'Alamgir, on the throne of Dehli.

Datta Sindhia

Datta Sindhia, Jankuji's uncle, about that time formed the design of invading the kingdom of the Rohillas; whereupon Najibu-d daula and other Rohilla chiefs, becoming cognizant of this fact, and perceiving the image of ultimate misfortune reflected in the mirror of the very beginning, wrote numerous letters to the Abdali Shah, and used every persuasion to induce him to come to Hindustan. The Shah, who was vexed at heart on account of Timur Shah and Jahan Khan having been compelled to take to flight, and was brooding over plans of revenge, accounted this friendly overture a signal advantage, and set himself at once in motion.

Datta, in company with his nephew Janku, after crossing the Juhna, advanced against Najibu-d daula, and 'Imadu-l Mulk, the *wazir*, hastened to Datta's support, agreeably to his request. As the number of the Mahratta troops amounted to nearly 80,000 horse, Najidu-d daula, finding his strength inadequate to risk an open battle, threw up intrenchments at Sakartal, one of the places belonging to Antarbed (the Doab), situated on the bank of the river Ganges, and there held himself in readiness to oppose the enemy. As the rainy season presented an insurmountable obstacle to Datta's movements, he was forced to suspend military operations, and in the interim Najibu-d daula despatched several letters to Nawab Shuja'u-d daula, begging his assistance.

The Nawab, urged by the promptings of valour and gallantry, started from Lucknow in the height of the rains, which fell with greater violence than in ordinary years, and having with the utmost spirit and resolution traversed the intervening roads, which were all in a wretched muddy condition, made Shahabad the site of his camp. Till the conclusion of the rainy season, however, he was unable to unite with Najibu-d daula, owing to the overflowing of the river Ganges.

No sooner had the rains come to an end, than one of the Mahratta chieftains, who bore the appellation of Gobind Pandit, forded the stream at Datta's command, with a party of 20,000 cavalry, and allowed no portion of Chandpur and many other populous places to escape conflagration and plunder. He then betook himself to the spot where Sa'du-llah Khan, Dundi Khan, and Hafiz Rahmat Khan had assembled, after having risen up in arms and quitted their abodes, to afford succour to Najibu-d daula. These three, finding themselves unable to cope with him, took refuge in the forests on the Kamaun hills.

Nawab Shuja'u-d daula, being apprised of this circumstance, mounted the fleet steed of resolution, and in Rabi'u-l awwal, 1173 A.H. (Oct. Nov. 1759 A.D.), taking his troops resembling the stars in his train, he repaired on the wings of speed to Chandpur, close to the locality where Najibu-d daula was stationed. As Gobind Pandit had reduced the latter's force as well as his companions to great straits, by cutting off their supply of provisions, Nawab Shuja'u-d daula Bahadur despatched 10,000 cavalry, consisting of Mughals and others, under the command of Mirza Najaf Khan Bahadur, Mir Bakar Himmati and other leaders, to attack the Pandit's camp. He also afterwards sent off Anupgar Gusain, and Raj Indar Gusain in rear of these. The leaders in question having fought with becoming gallantry, and performed the most valiant deeds, succeeded in routing the enemy. Out of the whole of Gobind Pandit's force, 200 were left weltering in blood, and as many more were captured alive, whilst a vast number were overwhelmed in the waters of the Ganges. Immense booty also fell into the hands of the victors, comprising every description of valuable goods, together with horses and cattle. Gobind Pandit, who after suffering this total defeat had escaped from the field of battle across the river Ganges, gave himself up to despair, and took to a precipitate flight. As soon as this intelligence reached the ears of Hafiz Rahmat Khan and the rest of the Rohilla chieftains, they sallied forth from the forests of Kamaun, and repaired to Nawab Shuja'u-d daula's camp. Meanwhile Najibu-d daula was released from the perils and misfortunes of his position.

Nawab Shuja'u-d daula Bahadur assembled the Rohilla chiefs, and offered them advice in the following strain: "The enemy has an innumerable army, his military prowess is formidable, and he has gained possession of most of the districts in your territory; it is therefore better for you to make overtures for peace." Every one, both high and low, applauded the Nawab's judicious counsel, and voted that pacific negotiations should be immediately entered into with Datta; but the truce had not yet been established on a secure basis, when the news of Ahmad Shah Abdali's approach, and of his arrival on this side of Lahore, astonished the ears of all. Datta, with the arrogance that ever filled his head, would not allow the preliminaries of peace to be brought to a conclusion; but haughtily discarding the amicable relations that he was in process of contracting, moved with a resolute step along the road to Dehli, with a view to encounter the Abdali Shah. He was accompanied at that time by 80,000 horsemen, well armed and equipped.

When the Shah set out from Lahore in the direction of Dehli, he thought to himself that on the direct road between these two places, owing to the passage to and fro of the Mahratta troops, it would be difficult to find any thriving villages, and grain and forage would be almost unprocurable. Consequently, in the month of Rabi'u-l awwal, 1173 A.H., he crossed the river Jumna, and entered Antarbed. Be it not unknown, that Antarbed is the name given to the land lying between the Ganges and Jumna, its frontier being Hardwar and the Kamaun hills, which are situated in the northern quarter of Hind....

In short, Ahmad Shah Durrani entered Antarbed, and Najibu-d daula and the other Rohilla chiefs, whose territories were situated in that kingdom, came to join the Shah. They likewise brought sums of money, as well as grain and provisions, to whatever extent they could procure them, and delivered them over the Shah's use. Through this cordial support of the Rohilla chiefs, the Shah acquired redoubled strength, and having directed his corps of Durranis, who were employed in the campaign on skirmishing duties, to pursue the ordinary route, and be in readiness for an engagement with Datta, proceeded himself to the eastward, by way of Antarbed.

On this side too, Datta, travelling with the speed of wind and lightning, conducted his army to Sirhind, where he happened to fall in with the Shah's skirmishing parties. As the Durranis are decidedly superior to the Mahratta troops in the rapidity of their evolutions, and in their system of predatory warfare, the moment they confronted each other, Datta's army was unable to hold its ground. Being compelled to give way, he retired to Dehli, keeping up a running fight all the way, and took up a position in the plain of Bawali, which lies in the vicinity of Shah-Jahanabad. At that juncture, Jankuji proposed to his nephew with haughty pride, that they should try and extricate themselves from their critical situation, and Jankuji at once did exactly what his respected uncle suggested. In fact, Datta and his troops dismounted from their horses after the manner of the inhabitants of Hind about to sacrifice their lives, and boldly maintained their footing on the field of battle. The Durranis assailed the enemy with arrows, matchlocks, and swords, and so overpowered them as not to allow a single individual to escape in safety from the scene of action. This event took place in Jumada-l awwal, 1173 A.H. (Jan. 1760 A.D.).

Malhar Rao Holkar

As soon as this intelligence reached the quick ear of Malhar Rao Holkar, who at that time was staying at Makandara, he consigned the surrounding districts to the flames, and making up his mind, proceeded in extreme haste to Suraj Mal Jat, and importuned that Raja to join him in the war against the Durrani Shah. The latter, however, strongly objected to comply with his request, stating that he was unable to advance out of his own territory to engage in hostilities with them, as he had not sufficient strength to risk a pitched battle; and that if the enemy were to make an attack upon him, he would seek refuge within his forts. In the interview, it came to Holkar's knowledge, that the Afghans of Antarbed had moved out of their villages with treasure and provisions, with intent to convey them to the Shah's camp, and had arrived as far as Sikandra, which is one of the dependencies of Antarbed, situated at a distance of twenty *kos* from Dehli towards the east. He consequently pursued them with the utmost celerity, and having fallen upon them, delivered them up to indiscriminate plunder.

The Abdali Shah, having been apprised of this circumstance, deputed Shah Kalandar Khan and Shah Pasand Khan Durrani, at the head of 15,000 horse, to chastise Holkar. The individuals in question, having reached Dehli from Narnaul, a distance of seventy *kos*, in twenty-four hours, and having halted during the day to recover from their fatigues, effected a rapid passage across the Jumna, as soon as half the night was over, and by using the utmost expedition, succeeded in reaching Sikandra by sunrise. They then encompassed Holkar's army, and made a vast number of his men fall a prey to their relentless swords. Holkar found himself reduced to great straits; he had not even sufficient leisure to fasten a saddle on his horse, but was compelled to mount with merely a saddle-cloth under him, and flee for his life. Three hundred more horsemen also followed after him in the same destitute plight, but the remainder of his troops, being completely hemmed in, were either slain or captured, and an immense quantity of property and household goods, as well as numbers of horses, fell into the hands of the Durranis. About this time, too, the Shah arrived at Dehli from Narnaul, and took up his quarters in the city.

Forces of the Dakhin

In the year 1172 A.H. (1758-9 A.D.), Raghunath Rao, the brother of Balaji Rao, after confiding the provinces of Lahore and Multan to Adina Beg Khan, and leaving Jankuji with a formidable army in the vicinity of the metropolis of Dehli, arrived at the city of Puna along with Shamsher Bahadur, Malhar Rao Holkar, and Jayaji Sindhiya. Sadasheo Rao Bhaoji, who was Balaji Rao's cousin, and his chief agent and prime minister, began instituting inquiries as to the receipts and disbursements made during the invasion of Hind. As soon as it became apparent, that after spending the revenue that had been levied from the country, and the proceeds arising from the plundered booty, the pay of the soldiery, amounting to about sixty *lacs* of rupees, was due; the vain illusion was dissipated from Bhaoji's brain. The latter's dislike to Raghunath Rao, moreover, had now broken into open contumely and discord, and Balaji Rao, vexed and disgusted 'at finding his own brother despised and disparaged, sent a letter to Bhaoji, declaring that it was essentially requisite for him now to unfurl the standard of invasion in person against Hindustan, and endure the fatigues of the campaign, since he was so admirably fitted for the undertaking. Bhao, without positively refusing to consent to his wishes, managed to evade compliance for a whole year, by having recourse to prevarication and subterfuge.

Biswas Rao, the son of Balaji Rao

Biswas Rao, Balaji Rao's eldest son, who was seventeen years old, solicited the command of the army from his father; and though the latter was in reality displeased with his request, yet in the year 1173 A.H. (1759-60 A.D.) he sent him off with Bhaoji in company. Malhar Rao, Pilaji Jadaun, Jan Rao Dhamadsari, Shamsher Bahadur, Sabuli Dadaji Rao, Jaswant Rao Bewar, Balwant Rao, Ganesh Rao, and other famous and warlike leaders, along with a force of 35,000 cavalry, were also associated with Bhao. Ibrahim Khan Gardi, who was the superintendent of the European artillery, likewise accompanied him. Owing to the extreme sultriness of the hot season, they were obliged to rest every other day, and thus by alternate marches and halts, they at length reached Gwalior.

'As soon as the story of 'Imadu-l Mulk and Jankuji Sindhia's having sought refuge in the forts belonging to Suraj Mal Jat, and the particulars of Datta's death and

Holkar's defeat, as well as the rout and spoliation of both their forces, were poured into the ears of Biswas Rao and Bhaoji by the reporters of news and the detailers of intelligence, vast excitement arose so that a sojourn of two months took place at Gwalior. Malhar Rao Holkar, who had escaped with his life from the battle with the Durranis, and in the mean time had joined Biswas Rao's camp, then started from Gwalior for Shah-Jahanabad by Bhao's order, at the head of a formidable army, and having reached Agra, took Jankuji Sindhia along with him from thence, and drew near to his destination.

Ahmad Shah Abdali, on ascertaining this news, sallied out from the city of Dehli to encounter him; but the latter, finding himself unable to resist, merely made some dashing excursions to the right and left for a few days, after the guerilla fashion. As the Shah, however, would never once refrain from pursuing him, he was ultimately forced to make an ignominious retreat back along the road he had come, and having returned to Gwalior, went and rejoined Bhaoji. The rainy season was coming on,. . . . so Ahmad Shah crossed the river Jumna, and having encamped at Sikandra, gave instructions to the officers of his army, to prepare houses of wood and grass for themselves, in place of tents and pavilions.

Bhao and Biswas Rao, having marched from Gwalior, after travelling many stages, and traversing long distances, as soon as they reached Akbarabad, Holkar and Jankuji, at Bhao's instigation, betook themselves to Raja Suraj Mal Jat, and brought him along with them to have an interview with Bhao. The latter went out a *kos* from camp to meet him, and 'Imadu-l Mulk, the *wazir*, also held a conference with Bhao through Suraj Mal's mediation. Suraj Mal proposed that the campaign should be conducted on the following plan, viz., that they should deposit their extra baggage and heavy guns, together with their female relatives, in the fort of Jhansi, by the side of the river Chambal; and then proceed to wage a predatory and desultory style of warfare against the enemy, as is the usual practice of the Mahratta troops; for under these circumstances their own territory would be behind their backs, and a constant supply of provisions would not fail to reach their camp in safety. Bhao and the other leaders, after hearing Suraj Mal's observations, approved of his decision; but Biswas Rao, who was an inexperienced youth, intoxicated with the wine of arrogance, would not follow his advice. Bhao accordingly carried on operations in conformity with Biswas Rao's directions, and set out from Akbarabad towards Dehli with the force that he had at his disposal. On Tuesday, the 9th of Zi-l hijja, 1173 A.H. (25 September 1760 A.D.), about the time of rising of the world-illumining sun, he enjoyed the felicity of beholding the fort of Dehli. The command of the garrision there was at that time entrusted to Ya'kub 'Ali Khan Bahmanzai, brother to Shah Wali Khan, the prime minister of the Durrani Shah; who, in spite of the multitude of his enemies, would not succumb, and spared no exertions to protect the fort with the few martial spirits that he had with him.

Capture of the fort of Dehli

Bhao, conjecturing that the fort of Dehli would be devoid of the protection of any garrision, and would therefore, immediately on being besieged, fall under his subjection, went and took up a position near Sa'du-llah Khan's mansion, with a multitude of troops. . . . Ibrahim Khan Gardi, who was a confederate of Bhao, and had the superintendence of the European artillery, planted his thundering cannon, with their skilful gunners, opposite the fort on the side of the sandy plain, and having made the battlements of the Octagon Tower and the Asad Burj a mark for his lightning-darting guns, overturned many of the royal edifices. Every day the tumultuous noise of attack on all sides of the fort filled the minds of the garrison with alarm and apprehension. The overflowing of the Jumna presented an insurmountable obstacle to the crossing of the Duranni Shah's army, and hindered it from affording any succour to the besieged. The provisions in the fort were very nearly expanded, and Ya'kub 'Ali Khan was forced to enter into negotiations for peace. He first removed, with his female relatives and property, from the fort to the domicile of 'Ali Mardan Khan, and then, having crossed the river Jumna from thence on board a boat, betook himself to the Shah's camp. On the 19th of the aforesaid month and year, Bhao entered the fort along with Biswas Rao, and took possession of all the property and goods that he could find in the old repositories of the royal family. He also broke in pieces the silver ceiling of the *Diwan-i Khass*, from which he extracted so much of the precious metal as to be able to coin seventeen *lacs* of rupees out of it. Narad Shankar Brahmin was then appointed by Bhao to the post of governor of the fort.

The Durrani Shah, after his engagement with Datta, which terminated in the destruction of the latter, had despatched Najibu-d daula to the province of Oudh with a conciliatory epistle, which was as it were a treaty of friendship, for the purpose of fetching Nawab Shuja'u-d daula Bahadur. Najibu-d daula accordingly betook himself by way of Etawa to Kanauj; and about the same time Nawab Shuja'd-d daula marched from Lucknow, and made the ferry of Mahdipur, which is one of the places in Etwa situated on this side the river Ganges, the site of his camp. An interview took place in that locality, and as soon as the friendly document had been perused, and the Nawab's heart had been comforted by its sincere promises, he came to the fixed determination of waiting on the Shah, and he sent back Raja Beni Bahadur, who at that time possessed greater power and influence than his other followers, to rule as viceroy over the kingdom during his absence. When Nawab Shuja'u-d daula approached the Shah's army, the prime minister, Shah Wali Khan, hastened out to meet him, and, having brought him along with him in the most courteous and respectful manner, afforded him the gratification, on the 4th of Zi-l hijja, 1173 A.H. (18th July, 1760 A.D.), of paying his respects to the Shah, and of folding the son of the latter, Timur Shah, in his embrace.

Bhao remained some time in the fort of Shah-Jahanabad, in consequence of the rainy season, which prevented the horses from stirring a foot, and deprived the cavalry of the power of fighting; he sent a person named Bhwani Sankar Pandit to Nawab Shuja'u-d daula, with the following message: "If it is inconvenient for you to contract an alliance with your friends, you should at least keep aloof from the enemy, and remain perfectly neutral to both parties." The above-named Pandit, having crossed the river Jumna, went to Nawab Shuja'u-d daula Bahadur, and delivered this message. The latter, after ascertaining its drift, despatched his eunuch Yakut Khan, who was one of the oldest and most confidential servants of his government, in company with Bhawani Shankar Pandit, and returned an answer of this description: "As the Rajas of this empire and the Rohilla chiefs were reduced to the last extremity by the violent aggressions of Raghunath Rao, Datta, Holkar, and their subordinates, they solicited the Abdali Shah to come to Hindustan, with the view of saving themselves from ruin. "The seed that they sowed has now begun to bear fruit.' Nevertheless, if peace be agreeable to you, from true regard for our ancient friendship, my best endeavours shall be used towards concluding one." Eventually, Bhao proposed that as far as Sirhind should be under the Shah's dominion, and all on this side of it should belong to him; but the whole rainy season was spent in negotiation, and no peace was established.

In the interim, Raja Suraj Mal Jat, who discerned the speedy downfall of the Mahratta power, having moved with his troops, in company with 'Imadu-l Mulk, the *wazir*, from his position at Sarai Badarpur, which is situated at a distance of six *kos* from Dehli on the eastern side, and traversed fifty *kos* in one night, without informing Bhao betook himself to Balamgarh,⁵ which is one of his forts.

As the Mahratta troops made repeated complaints to Bhao regarding the scarcity of grain and forage, the latter, on the 29th of the month of Safar, 1174 A.H. (9th October, 1760 A.D.), removed Shah Jahan, son of Muhi'u-s Sunnat, son of Kam Bakhsh, son of Aurangzeb 'Alamgir, and having seated the illustrious Prince, Mirza Jawan Bakht, the grandson of 'Alamgir II., on the throne of Dehli, publicly conferred the dignity of *wazir* on Shuja'u-d daula. His object was this, that the Durrani Shah might become averse to and suspicious of the Nawab in question. Leaving Narad Shankar Brahmin, of whom mention has been made above, behind in the fort of Shah-Jahanabad, he himself set out, with all his partisans and retainers, in the direction of Kunjpura.⁶ This place is fifty-four *kos* to the west of Dehli, and seven to the north of the *pargana* of Karnal, and it is a district the original cultivators of which were the Rohillas.

Capture of the fort of Kunjpura

Bhao, on the 10th of Rabi'u-l awwal, 1174 A.H. (19th October, 1760), encompassed the fort of Kunjpura with his troops, and subdued it in the twinkling of an eye by the fire of his thundering cannon. Several chiefs were in the fort, one of whom was 'Abdu-s Samad Khan Abdali, governor of Sirhind, who had been taken prisoner by Raghunath Rao in 1170 A.H. (1756-7), but had ultimately obtained his release, as was related in the narrative of Adina Beg Khan's proceedings. There were, besides, Kutb Khan Rohilla, Dalil Khan, and Nijabat Khan, all *zamindars* of places in Antarbed, who had been guilty of conveying supplies to the Abdali Shah's camp. After reducing the fort, Bhao made 'Abdu-s Samad Khan and

⁵ ["*To Dig.*"—*Nigar-nama-i Hind.*]
⁶ ["*A stout and substantial stronghold containing a garrison of nearly 30,000 men.*"—*Nigar-nama-i Hind.*]

Kutb Khan undergo capital punishment, and kept the rest in confinement; whilst he allowed Kunjpura itself to be sacked by his predatory hordes.

As soon as this intelligence reached the Shah's ear, the sea of his wrath was deeply agitated; and notwithstanding that the stream of the Jumna had not yet subsided sufficiently to admit of its being forded, a royal edict was promulgated, directing his troops to pay no regard to the current, but cross at once from one bank to the other. As there was no help but to comply with this mandate, on the 16th of the month of Rabi'u-l awwal, 1174 A.H. (25th October, 1760 A.D.), near Shah-Jahanabad, on the road to Pakpat, which is situated fifteen *kos* to the north of Dehli, they resigned themselves to fate, and succeeded in crossing. A number were swallowed up by the waves, and a small portion of the baggage and quadrupeds belonging to the army was lost in the passage. As soon as the intelligence reached Bhao's ear, that a party of Durranis had crossed, . . . he sounded the drum of retreat from Kunjpura, and with his force of 40,000 well-mounted and veteran cavalry, and a powerful train of European artillery, under the superintendence of Ibrahim Khan Gardi, he repaired expeditiously to Panipat, which lies forty *kos* from Dehli towards the west.

Battle between the Mahratta Army and the Durranis

The abdali Shah, after crossing the river Jumna at the *ghat* of Pakpat, proceeded in a westerly direction, and commanded that Nawab Shuja'u-d daula Bahadur and Najibu-d daula should pitch their tents on the left of the royal army; and Dundi Khan, Hafizu-l Mulk Hafiz Rahmat Khan, and Ahmad Khan Bangash on the right. As Bhao perceived that it was difficult to contend against the Durranis in the open field, by the advice of his counsellors he made a permanent encampment of his troops in the outskirts of the city of Panipat, and having intrenched it all round with his artillery, took up his quarters in this formidable position. . . .

In the interim Gobind Pandit, who was the *tahsildar* of the district of Shukohabad, etc., betook himself to Dehli at Bhao's suggestion, with a body of 10,000 cavalry, and intercepted the transport of supplies to the Durrani Shah's army.[7] ...

When the basis of the enemy's power had been overthrown (at Panipat), and the surface of the plain had been relieved of the insolent foe, the triumphant champions of the victorious army proceeded eagerly to pillage the Mahratta camp, and succeeded in gaining possession of an unlimited quantity of silver and jewels, 500 enormous elephants, 50,000 horses, 1000 camels, and two *lacs* of bullocks with a vast amount of goods and chattels, and a countless assortment of camp equipage. Nearly 30,000 labourers too, who drew their origin from the Dakhin, fell into captivity. Towards evening the Abdali Shah went out to look at the bodies of the slain, and found great heaps of corpses, and running streams produced by the flood of gore. ... Thirty-two mounds of slain were counted, and the ditch, protected by artillery, of such immense length that it could contain several *lacs* of human beings, besides cattle and baggage, was completely filled with dead bodies.

Assassination of Sindhia Jankuji

Rao Kashi Nath, on seeing Jankuji, who was a youth of twenty, with a handsome countenance, and at that time had his wounded hand hanging in a sling from his neck, became deeply grieved, and the tears started from his eyes.... Jankuji raised his head and exclaimed: "It is better to die with one's friends than to live among one's enemies."

The Nawab, in unison with Shah Wali Khan, solicit-

---

[7] *For accounts of the skirmishes and battle see the previous volume ("Studies in Indian History", Part II). This work is more diffuse, and enters into greater details, but the two accounts agree in the main.*

ted the Shah to spare Jankuji's life; whereupon, the Shah summoned Barkhurdar Khan, and consulted him on the propriety of the step, to which the Khan in question returned a decided negative. At the same time, one of the Durranis, at Barkhurdar Khan's suggestion, went and cut Jankuji's throat, and buried him under ground inside the very tent in which he was imprisoned.

Ibrahim Khan Gardi's Death

Shuja'u Kuli Khan, a powerful and influential servant of the Nawab Shuja'u-d daula Bahadur, having captured Ibrahim Khan Gardi on the field of battle, kept him with the said Nawab's cognizance in his own tent. No sooner did this intelligence become public, than the Durranis began in a body to raise a violent tumult, and clamorously congregating round the door of the Shah's tent, declared that Ibrahim Gardi's neck was answerable for the loss of so many thousands of their fellow-countrymen, and that whoever sought to protect him would incur the penalty of their resentment. Nawab Shuja'u-d daula, feeling that one seeking refuge cannot be slain, prepared for a contest with the Durrani forces, whereupon there ensued a fraightful disturbance. At length, Shah Wali Khan took Nawab Shuja'd-d daula aside privately, and addressing him in a friendly and affectionate tone, proposed, that he should deliver up Ibrahim Khan Gardi to him, for the sake of appeasing the wrath of the Durranis; and after a week, when their evil passions had been allayed, he would restore to him the individual entrusted to his care. In short, Ashrafu-l Wuzra (Shah Wali Khan), having obtained him from the Nawab, applied a poisonous plaster to his wounds; so that, by the expiration of a week, his career was brought to a close.

Discovery of Bhaoji's Corpse

The termination of Bhaoji's career has been differently related. Nawab Shuja'u-d daula, having mounted after the victory, took Shisha Dhar Pandit, Ganesh Pandit, and other associates of Bhaoji along with him, and began wandering over the field of battle, searching for the corpses of the Mahratta chiefs, and more especially for Bhaoji's dead body. They accordingly recognized the persons of Jaswant Rao Balwar, Pilaji, and Sabhaji Nath who had received forty sword-cuts, lying on the scene of action; and, in like manner, those of other famous characters also came in view. Bhao's corpse had not been found, when from beneath a dead body three valuable gems unexpecteadly shone forth. The Nawab presented those pearls to the Pandits mentioned above, and directed them to try and recognize that lifeless form. They succeeded in doing so through the scar of a gunshot wound in the foot, and another on the side behind the back, which Bhao had received in former days. With their eyes bathed in tears they exclaimed: "This is Bhao, the ruler of the Dakhin."* Some entertain an opinion, that Bhao, after Biswas Rao's death, performed prodigies of valour, and then disappeared from sight, and no one ever saw him afterwards. Tho individuals consequently, both natives of the Dakhin, have publicly assumed the name of Bhao, and dragged a number of people into their deceitful snare. As a falsehood cannot bear the light, one was eventually put to death somewhere in the Dakhin by order of the chiefs in that quarter; and the other, having excited an insurrection at Benares, was confined for some time in the fort of Chunar. After his release, despairing of the success of his project, he died in the suburbs of Gorakhpur in the year 1193 A.H.

Nawab Shuja'u-d daula Bahadur, having obtained permission of the Shah to burn the bodies [*of the Bhao and other chiefs*], deputed Raja Himmat Bahadur and Rao Kashi Nath, his principal attendants, to perform the task of cremation. Out of all those hapless and unfortunate beings [*who survived the battle*], a number

*[The *Nigar-nama-i Hind* gives further identifications of the corpse.]

maintained a precarious existence against the violent assaults of death for some days; but notwithstanding that they used the most strenuous exertions to effect their escape in divers directions from Panipat, not a single one was saved from being slain and plundered by the *zamindars* of that quarter. Out of the whole of the celebrated chiefs too, with the exception of Malhar Rao Holkar, 'Appaji Gaikawar and Bithal Sudeo, not another was ever able to reach the Dakhin.

Account of Bhaoji's Wife

Bhao's wife, in company with Shamsher Bhadur, half-brother* to Balaji Rao, and a party of confidential attendants, traversed a long distance with the utmost celerity, and betook herself to the fortress of Dig. There that broken-hearted lady remained for two or three days mourning the loss of her husband, and having then made up her mind to prepare for an expedition to the Dakhin, Raja Suraj Mal Jat gave her one morning a suitable escort to attend her, and bade her adieu. She accordingly reached the Dakhin; but Shamsher Bahadur, who was severely wounded, died after arriving at Dig.

Death of Balaji

Shortly before the occurrence of these disasters, Balaji Rao had marched from Poona. He had only proceeded as far as Bhilsa, when, having been informed of the event, he grew tired of existence, and shed tears of blood lamenting the loss of a son and a brother. He then moved from where he was to Sironj, and about that very time a messenger reached him from the Abdali Shah, with a mourning *khil'at*. The Rao, feigning obedience to his commands, humbly dressed his person in the Shah's *khil'at* and turning away from Sironj, re-entered Poona.

*[He was the illegitimate son of Baji Rao by a Muhammad woman, and he was brought up as a Muhammadan.]

From excesses of grief and woe, however, he remained for two months afflicted with a harrowing disease; and as he preceived the image of death reflected from the mirror of his condition, he sent for his brother, Raghunath Rao, to whom he gave in charge his best beloved son, the younger brother of the lately slain Biswas Rao, who bore the name of Madhu Rao, and had just entered his twelfth year, exclaiming: "Fulfil all the duties of goodwill towards this fatherless child, treating him as if he were your own son, and do not permit any harm to come upon him." Having said this, he departed from the world on the 9th of Zi-l ka,da, 1174 A.H. (14th June, 1761 A.D.), and the priod of his reign was twenty-one years.

Madhu Rao, son of Balaji

Madhu Rao, after the demise of his father, was installed in the throne of sovereignty at Poona; and Raghunath Rao conducted the administration of affairs as prime minister, after the manner of the late Bhao.

Account of the pretender Bhao

One of the remarkable incidents that occurred in Madhu Rao's reign was the appearance of a counterfeit Bhao, who, in the year 1175 A.H. (1762-3 A.D.), having induced a number of refractory characters to flock to his standard, and having collected together a small amount of baggage and effects, with camp equipage and cattle, excited an insurrection near the fort of Karaza, which is situated at a distance of twelve *kos* from Jhansi towards the west. He gave intimation to the governor of the fort, who held his appointment of the Poona chiefs, as to his name and pretensions, and summoned him by threats and promises into his presence. The latter, who, up to that time, had been in doubt whether Bhao was dead or alive, being apprehensive lest this individual should in reality prove to be Bhao, proceeded to wait upon him, and presented some cash and valuables by way of offering. After that, the Bhao in question sent letters into other *parganas*, and having summoned the revenue officers from all quarters, commenced seizing and appropriating all the cash, property and goods. Whatever horses, elephants or camels he found with any one, he immediately sent for, and kept in his own possession.

This pretender to the name of Bhao always kept his face half covered under a veil, both in public and private, on the plea that the wound on his visage was still unhealed, and people were completely deceived by the stratagem; no one could have the impudence to scrutinize his features. In short, for six months he persevered in his imposture until the news reached Poona, when some spies went over to him to examine strictly into the case, and discovered that he was not Bhao.

About the same period, Malhar Rao Holkar was moving from the Dakhin towards Hindustan, and his road happened to lie through the spot where the pretender in question had pitched his tents. The above-mentioned spies disclosed the particulars of the case to Malhar Rao, who thought to himself, that until Parbati Bai, the late Bhao's wife, had seen this individual with her own eyes, and all her doubts had been removed, it would not do to inflict capital punishment on the impostor, for fear the lady should think in her heart that he had killed her husband out of spite and malice. For this reason, Malhar Rao merely took the impostor prisoner, and having appointed thirty or forty horsemen to take care of him, forwarded him from thence to Poona. The few weak-minded beings, who had gathered round him, were allowed to depart to their several homes, and Holkar proceeded to his destination. When the pretender was brought to Poona, Madhu Rao likewise, out of regard for the feelings of the late Bhao's wife, deemed it proper to defer his execution, and kept him confined in one of the forts within his own dominions. Strange to say, the silly people in that fort did not discover the falseness of the impostor's claims, and leagued themselves with him.

so that a fresh riot was very nearly being set on foot. Madhu Rao, however, having been apprised of the circumstances, despatched him from that fort to another stronghold; and in the same way his removal and transfer was constantly taking place from various forts in succession, till he was finally confined in a stronghold, that lies contiguous to the sea on the island of Kolaba, which is a dependency of the Kokan territory.

Nawab Nizam 'Ali Khan Bahadur

The following is another of the events of Madhu Rao's reign: Bithal, *diwan* of Nawab Nizam 'Ali Khan Bahadur, advised his master, that as the Mahrattas were then devoid of influence, and the supreme authority was vested in an inexperienced child, it would be advisable to ravage Poona. Januji Bhonsla Raja of Nagpur, Gopal Rao a servant of the Peshwa, and some more chiefs of the Mahratta nation, approved of the *diwan's* suggestion, and led their forces in a compact mass towards Poona. When they drew near its frontier, Raghunath Rao, who was Madhu Rao's chief agent and prime minister, got terrified at the enemy's numbers, and finding himself incompetent to cope with them, retired with his master from Puna. Nawab Nizam 'Ali Khan Bahadur then entered the city, and did not spare any efforts in completing its destruction.

After some time, Raghunath Rao recovered himself, and having entered into friendly communication with Januji Bhonsla and the other chiefs of his own tribe, by opening an epistolary correspondence with them, he alienated the minds of these men from the Nawab. In short, the above-named chiefs separated from the Nawab on the pretence of its being the rainy season, and returned to their own territories. In the interim, Raghunath Rao and Madhu Rao set out to engage Nawab Nizam 'Ali Khan Bahadur, who, deeming it expedient to proceed to his original quarters, beat a retreat from the position he was occupying. When the bank of the river

Godavari became the site of his encampment, an order was issued for the troops to cross over. Half the *materiel* of the army was still on this side, and half on that; when Raghunath, considering it a favourable opportunity, commenced a furious onslaught. The six remaining chiefs of the Nawab's army were slain, and about 7,000 Afghans, etc., acquired eternal renown by gallantly sacrificing their lives. After this sanguinary conflict, the Nawab hastily crossed the river, and extricated himself from his perilous position. As soon as the flame of strife had been extinguished, a peace was established through the intervention of Malhar Rao Holkar, who had escaped with his life in safety from the battle with Abdali Shah. Both parties concurring in the advantages of an amicable understanding, returned to their respective quarters.

Quarrel between Raghunath Rao and Madhu Rao
When Raghunath Rao began to usurp greater authority over the administration of affairs, Gopika Bai, Madhu Rao's mother, growing envious of his influence, inspired her son with evil suspicions against him, and planned several stratagems, whereby their mutual friendship might result in hatred and animosity, till at length Raghunath Rao became convinced that he would some day be imprisoned. Consequently, he mounted his horse one night, and fled precipitately from Poona with only a few adherents. Stopping at Nasik, which lies at a distance of eight stages from Poona, he fixed upon that town as his place of refuge and abode, and employed himself in collecting troops; insomuch that Naradji Sankar, the revenue collector of Jhansi, Jaswant Rao Lud, Sakha Ram Bapu and Nilkanth Mahadeo, volunteered to join him, and eagerly engaged in active hostilities against Madhu Rao. As soon as Raghunath Rao arrived in this condition close to Poona, Madhu Rao was also obliged to sally forth from it in company with Trimbak Rao, Bapuji Manik, Gopal Rao and Bhimji Lamdi. When the line of battle began to be formed, Raghunath Rao assumed

the initiative in attacking his adversaries, and succeeded in routing Madhu Rao's force by a series of overwhelming assaults; and even captured the Rao himself, together with Nar Singh Rao. After gaining this agreeable victory, as he perceived Madhu Rao to be in safety, and his malicious antagonists overthrown, he could not contain himself for joy. As soon as he returned from the battlefield to his encampment, he seated Madhu Rao on a throne, and remained himself standing in front of him, after the manner of slaves. By fawning and coaxing, he then removed every trace of annoyance from Madhu Rao's mind, and requested him to return to Poona. After dismissing him to that city, he himself went with his retinue and soldiery to Nasik.

Haidar Naik

After the lapse of some years of Madhu Rao's reign, a vast disturbance arose in the Dakhin. Haidar Naik having assembled some bold and ferocious troops, . . . with intent to subdue the territory of the Mahrattas, set out in the direction of Poona. Madhu Rao came from Poona, and summoned Raghunath Rao to his assistance from Nasik, whereupon the latter joined him with a body of 20,000 of his cavalry. In short, they marched with their combined forces against the enemy; and on several occasions encounters took place, in which the lives of vast multitudes were destroyed. Although Haidar Naik's army proved themselves superior in the field, yet peace was ultimately concluded on the cession and surrender of some few tracts in the royal dominions; after which Haidar Naik refrained from hostilities, and returned to his own territory; whilst Madhu Rao retired to Poona, and Raghunath Rao to Nasik.

Raghunath Rao's Movements

When a short time had elapsed after this, the idea of organizing the affairs of Hindustan entered into Raghu Rao's mind. For the sake of preserving outward propriety, therefore, he first gave intimation to Madhu Rao of his intention, and asked his sanction. The Rao in question, who did not feel himself secure from Raghunath Rao, and considered any increase to his power a source of great weakness to himself, addressed him a reply couched in these terms: "It were better for you to remain where you are, in the enjoyment of repose."... Raghunath Rao would not listen to these words, but marched out of Nasik in company with Mahaji Sindhia, taking three powerful armies along with him.

As soon as he reached Gwalior, he commenced hostilities against Rana Chattar Singh, who possessed all the country round Gohad, and laid siege to the town itself. Godh is the name of a city, founded by the aforesaid Rana. It is fortified with earthen towers and battlements, and is situated eighteen *kos* from Gwalior. Madhu Rao, during the continuance of the siege, kept constantly sending messages to Rana Chattar Singh, telling him to persist in his opposition to Raghunath with a stout heart, as the army of the Dakhin should not be despatched to his kingdom to reinforce the latter. In a word, for the period of a year they used the most arduous endeavours to capture Gohad, but failed in attaining their object. During this campaign, the sum of thirty-two *lacs* of rupees, taken from the pay of the troops and the purses of the wealthy bankers, was incurred by Raghunath Rao as a debt to be duly repaid. He then returned to the Dakhin distressed and overwhelmed with shame, and entered the city of Nasik, wither Madhu Rao also repaired about the same time, to see and inquire after his fortunes. In the course of the interview, he expressed the deepest regret for the toils and disappointment that the Rao had endured, and ultimately returned in haste to Poona, after thus sprinkling salt on the galling wound. Shortly after this, Kankuma Tantia and his other friends persuaded Raghunath Rao to adopt a Brahmin's son.... Accordingly the Rao attended to the advice of his foolish counsellors, and selected an individual for adoption. He constituted Amrat Rao his heir.

Raghunath Rao's Imprisonment At Poona

Madhu Rao no sooner became cognizant of this fact, than he felt certain that Raghunath Rao was meditating mischief and rebellion, and seeking to usurp a share in the sovereignty of the realm. He consequently set out for Nasik with a force of 25,000 horsemen, whilst, on the other hand, Raghunath Rao also organized his troops, and got ready for warfare. Just about that period, however, Kankuma Tantia and Takuji Holkar,[10] who were two of the most powerful and influential men in Raghunath's army, declared to him that it was necessary for them to respect their former obligations to Madhu Rao, and therefore improper to draw the sword upon him. After a long altercation, they left the Rao where he was, and departed from Nasik. Raghunath, from the paucity of his troops, not deeming it advantageous to fight, preferred enduring disgrace, and fled with 2000 adherents to the fort of Dhudhat.[11]

Madhu Rao then entered Nasik, and commenced sequestrating his property and imprisoning his partisans; after which he pitched his camp at the foot of the above-named fort, and placed Raghunath in a most precarious position. For two or three days the incessant discharge of artillery and musketry caused the flames of war to blaze high, but pacific negotiations were subsequently opened, and a firm treaty of friendship entered into, whereupon the said Rao came down from the fort, and had an interview with Madhu Rao. The latter then placed his head upon the other's feet, and asked pardon for his offences. Next day, having mounted Raghunath

---

[10][*These names are very doubtful in the MS. The latter one is no doubt intended for Tukaji.*]

[11][*"Dhoorup, a fort in the Chandor range."—Grant Duff, vol. ii. p. 199.*]

Rao on his own private elephant, he himself occupied the seat usually assigned to the attendants, and continued for several days travelling in this fashion the distance to Poona. As soon as they entered Poona, Madhu Rao, imitating the behavious of an inferior to a superior, exceeded all bounds in his kind and consoling attentions towards Raghunath Rao. After that he selected a small quantity of goods and a moderate equipment of horses and elephants, out of his own establishment, and having deposited them all together in one of the most lofty and spacious apartments, solicited Raghunath Rao in a respectful manner to take up his abode there. The latter then became aware of his being a prisoner with the semblance of freedom, and reluctantly complied with Madhu Rao's requisition.

Raja of Nagpur

As soon as Madhu Rao had delivered his mind from all apprehension regarding Raghunath Rao, he led his army in the direction of Nagpur, in order to avenge himself on Januji Bhonsla, the Raja of that place, who had been an ally and auxiliary of Raghunath Rao, in one of his engagements. The Raja in question, not finding himself capable of resisting him, fled from his original residence; so that for a period of three months Madhu Rao was actively engaged in pursuing his adversary, and that unfortunate outcast from his native land was constantly fleeing before him. Ultimately, having presented an offering of fifteen *lacs* of rupees, he drew back his foot from the path of flight, and set out in safety and security for his own home.

Madhu Rao's Death

After chastising the Raja of Nagpur, Madhu Rao entered Poona with immense pomp and splendour, and amused himself with gay and festive entertainments. But he was attacked with a fatal disease, and . . . his life was in danger. On one occasion he laid his head on Raghunath Rao's feet, and. . . . asked forgiveness for the faults of bygone days. Raghunath Rao grieved deeply on account of his youth... He applied himself zealously to the cure of the invalid, and whenever he found a trace, in any quarter or direction, of austere Brahmins and skilful Pandits, he sent for them to administer medicines for his recovery. At length, when the sick man began to despair of living, he imitated the example of his deceased father, and placed his younger brother, whose name was Narain Rao, under the charge of Raghunath Rao, and having performed the duty of recommending him to his care, yielded up his soul in the year 1186 A.H (1772 A.D.). The duration of his reign was twelve years.

Narain Rao, Son of Balaji Rao

Narain Rao, after being seated on the throne of sovereignty, owing to his tender age, committed various acts that produced an ill-felling among his adherents, both great and small, at Poona; more especially in Raghunath Rao, on whom he inflicted unbecoming indiginities. Although Madhu Rao had not behaved towards his uncle with the respect due to such a relative, yet, beyond this much, that he would not grant him permission to move away from Poona, he had treated him with no other incivility; but used always, till the day of his death, to show him the atention due from an inferior to a superior; and supplied him with wealth and property far exceeding the limits of his wants. In short, Raghunath Rao, having begun to form plans for taking Narain Rao prisoner, first disclosed his secret to Sakha Ram Bapu, who was Madhu Rao's prime minister, and having seduced that artless courtier from his allegiance, made him an accomplice in his treacherous designs. Secondly, having induced Kharak Singh and Shamsher Singh, the chiefs of the body of Gardis, to join his conspiracy, he raised the standard of insurrection. Accordingly, those two faithless wretches one day, under the pretence of deman-

9.

ding pay for the troops, made an assault on the door of Narain Rao's apartment, and reduced him to great distress. That helpless being, who had not the slightest cognizance of the deceitful stratagems of the conspirators, despatched a few simple-minded adherents to oppose the insurgents, and then stealthily repaired to Raghunath Rao's house. Kharak Singh and Shamsher Singh, being apprised of the circumstance, hurried after him, and, unsheathing their swords, rushed into Raghunath Rao's domicile. Raghunath Rao first fell wounded in the affray, and subsequently Narain Rao was slain. This event took place in the year 1187 A.H., so that the period of Narain Rao's reign was one year.

Reign of Raghunath Rao

Kharak Singh and Shamsher Singh, through whose brains the fumes of arrogance had spread, in consequence of their control over the whole train of European artillery, with wilful and headstrong insolence seated Raghunath Rao on the throne of sovereignty, without the concurrence of the other chiefs; and the said Rao continued to live for two months at Puna after the manner of rightful rulers. After Narain Rao had been put to death, a certain degree of shame and remorse came over the Puna chiefs, and the dread of their own overthrow entered their minds. Sakha Ram Bapu consequently, in unison with Trimbak Rao, commonly called Matamadhari Balhah,[12] and others, deemed it advisable to persuade Raghunath Rao that he should go forth from Puna, and employ himself in settling the kingdom. The said Rao accordingly acted upon their suggestion, and marched out of Poona, attended by the Mahratta chiefs. As soon as he had got to the distance of two or three stages from the city, the wily chiefs, by alleging some excuse, obtain-

---

[12][*Grant Duff calls him "Trimbuck Rao Mama." The word transcribed from the MS. as "Balhah" is very doubtful.*]

ed leave from Raghunath Rao to return, and repaired from the camp to the city. They then summoned to them in private all the commanders of the army, both great and small; when they came to the unanimous decision, that it was incompatible with justice to acquiesce in Raghunath Rao's being invested with the supreme authority, and that it would be better, as Narain Rao's wife was six months advanced in pregnancy, providing she gave birth to a male child, to invest that infant with the sovereignty, and conduct the affairs of government agreeably to the details of prudence. As soon as they had unanimously settled the question after this fashion, a few of the chiefs took up a position in the outskirts of the city of Poona, by way of protection, and formed a sturdy barrier against the Magog of turbulence. Raghunath Rao, having become aware of the designs of the conspirators, remained with a slender party in his encampment. Having brooded over his troubles, he saw no remedy left but that of forsaking the country, and was consequently forced to retire towards the Carnatic. His object was to collect a sufficient force round him, with which he might return to Poona and resume hostilities. However, owing to the vulgar report that attributed Narain Rao's murder to him, every blade of grass that sprung from the ground was ready to plunge a dagger into his blood. For this reason, he found it impossible either to stay or reside in the Carnatic, so he hastened away to Surat.

Death of the pretender Bhao

The direst confusion had found its way into the kingdom, in consequence of the report of Narain Rao's death. At that critical juncture the pretender Bhao, who was confined in a stronghold in the Kokan territory, lying adjacent to the salt ocean, seized the opportunity of escaping by fraud and stratagem out of his prison, and having induced a party of men to place themselves under his orders, took possession of some of the forts and districts of that country. He was just on the point of waging open war, had not Mahaji Sindhia Bahadur set out in the interim from Puna to the Kokan territory for the purpose of coercing him. On reaching his destination, he engaged in hostilities with the aforesaid Bhao, whereupon the latter's associates took to flight, and departed each by his own road. As Bhao was thus left alone, he went on board a ship in utter consternation with a view to save his life from that vortex of perdition; but death granted him no respite, and he fell alive into the hands of the heroes who accompanied Mahaji Sindhia Bahadur. The latter brought him along with him to Poona, and removed the dust of uncertainty from the mirror of every mind. Ultimately he caused the ill-fated wretch to be bound to a camel's foot, and paraded round the whole town; after which he put him to death.

Sawai Madhu Rao, son of Narain Rao, surnamed the Peshwa Sahib

The Peshwa Sahib, the rightful heir of Narain Rao, at the time of his father's murder, was dwelling in his mother's womb. . . . When she had completed the time of her pregnancy, a child, in the year 1188 A.H. (1774 A.D.), shed a grace over the bosom of its nurse, and bestowed comfort on the illustrious chiefs. . . . He was invested with the appellation of Sawai Madhu Rao.

Advance of the English Commanders upon Poona

Raghunath Rao, having reached Surat, turned towards the leaders of the English army, who dwelt on the borders of the sea, and offered to take upon himself the responsibility of showing the way over the various routes into the Dakhin, and to subjugate that kingdom so teeming with difficulties. As the commanders of the English army were possessed of adequate means for making an invasion, and had their heads inflamed with the intoxication of boldness and intrepidity, they took Raghunath Rao along with them, and moving away from Surat with their valiant troops experienced in war, and their lion-hearted forces active as tigers, they set out to conquer and annex the Dakhin territories.

Having traversed the intervening stages at a resolute pace, they arrived at Nurghat, which is situated at a distance of twenty *kos* from Poona. The Mahratta chieftains also sallied forth from Poona with a vast body of retainers, and opposed their advance with the utmost perseverance at Nurghat; whereupon a tremendous contest and a frightful slaughter ensued, until the combatants on both sides had neither the power nor the inclination left to assail each other any more. At length, by the intervention of the obscurity of night, the tumult of war subsided, and the world-consuming fire of guns and matchlocks, whose flames arose to the highest heavens, hid its face in the ashes of night so that the soldiery on either side were obliged to retire to their respective quarters. During that night, the prudent belligerents made up their minds to a peace; and in the morning, the chiefs of the rival forces obtained an interview and enjoyed a conference. The English leaders, after negotiating a truce and consolidating the basis of friendship, delivered up Raghunath Rao, who had been the instigator of this conflict and the originator of this hostile movement, to the Mahratta chiefs, on condition of their granting him a *jagir*, and treating him with kindness and consideration. They then turned away from that quarter with all their troops and followers, and repaired to their usual place of abode.

The Mahratta chiefs had formed the fixed determination in their minds of taking vengeance on the ill-fated Raghunath Rao; but Mahaji Sindhia Bahadur, prompted by his manly and generous feelings, diverted them from their headlong and cruel purposes, so that the matter was managed mercifully and kindly, and the Rao in question, having been presented with a *jagir*, received permission to remain at large. The unfortunate wretch, however, departed from the pleasant vale of existence to the desert of non-entity, without reaching his destination, for the career of the wicked never ends well.

Mahaji Sindhia Bahadur

When the fourth year from the birth of Sawai Madhu Rao, surnamed the Peshwa Sahib, had elapsed, and security and repose had settled on the minds of high and low throughout the territories of the Dakhin, Mahaji Sindhia Bahadur, who was distinguished among all the Poona chiefs for his gallantry and daring, sagacity and intelligence, having satisfied his mind as to the settlement of that kingdom, set out to conquer Gohad. He succeeded in taking prisoner Rana Chattar Singh, who was in the citadel, after a siege attended with hard fighting, and took possession of the surrounding districts, along with the fortress of Gwalior, which is a mountain stronghold.

About the same time, a mutual feeling of envy and hatred had become firmly implanted in the minds of Mirza Muhammad Shafi' Khan and Muhammad Beg Khan Hamadani,—who 'had been the chief officers of State to the late Amiru-l umara Mirza Najaf Khan Bahadur, and after his death had been partners in the government of the province of Agra,—owing to their each craving after an increase of power and dignity, which is ever a hindrance to the existence of friendship and good feeling among equals and contemporaries. At last, Muhammad Beg Khan Hamadani seized the opportunity, during an interview, of putting Muhammad Shafi' Khan to death; and on this account, Afrasiyab Khan, who was the Imperial *Mir-i atish*, and one of Amiru-l umara Mirza Najaf Khan Bahadur's *proteges*, becoming alarmed, demanded succour of Mahaji Sindhia Bahadur. The latter had firmly resolved in his mind on repairing to the sublime threshold, but had not yet fulfilled the duty of paying his respects, when, under the influence of Sindhia Bahadur's destiny, Afrasiyab Khan was killed by the hand of an assassin.

Sindhia Bahadur's army having overshadowed the

metropolis by its arrival, he brought Muhammad Beg Khan Hamadani, after a siege, completely under his subjection, and in the year 1199 A.H. traversed the streets of the metropolis. When he obtained the good fortune of saluting the threshold . . . of His Majesty, the shadow of God, the Emperor Shah 'Alam, . . . he was loaded with princely favours, and distinguished by royal marks of regard, so that he became the chief of the supporters of government, and His Majesty's most staunch and influential adherent. . . .

As Madhu Rao, the Peshwa Sahib, at the present auspicious period, pursues, in contradistinction to his uncle, the path of obedience to the monarch of Islam, and Mahaji Sindhia Bahadur is one of those who are constantly attached to the ever-triumphant train, hence it happens that the plant of this nation's prosperity has struck root firmly into the earth of good fortune, and their affairs flourish agreeably to their wishes.

LUBBU-S SIYAR
OF
ABU TALIB LONDONI

This is a very useful little manual of general history, compiled in 1208 A.H. (1793-4 A.D.), by Mirza Abu Muhammad Tabrizi Isfahani, and being carried down to modern times, embraces an account of Europe and America.

The author is usually known in India as Abu Talib Londoni, from his voyage to and adventures in England and Europe, an amusing account of which was written by him on his return in 1803, and is well known to the European world by the translation of Major Stewart.

In the Preface to this work he tells us that he had collected several works of history and travel, and had often perused them, but found amongst them none that contained a history of the whole world; he therefore thought that he would himself supply this deficiency, but had no leisure to effect his object till the year above mentioned, when he finished his Abstract. He declares his intention, if he lives long enough, of enlarging his work, and hopes that some one else, if he fails to do it, will undertake this useful labour, "because he has mentioned all the occurrences of the world, old and new, and given a connected account of the Prophets, Khalifs, Sultans, and celebrated men, from the beginning to the present time."

He quotes the various authorities he used, and besides others of common note, he mentions a history of the Kings of India compiled by himself, and a compendious account of the kingdoms of Europe and America, translated by some English gentleman from his own tongue, "which in truth contains very many new matters." This is no doubt the work of Jonathan Scott. He says that his own history is an abstract of some thousands of books, and therefore he has entitled it *Lubbu-s Siyar wa Jahannuma*, "The Essence of Biographies, and the World-Reflecting Mirror."

The author was the son of Haji Muhammad Khan, a Turk of Azurbaijan, who was bron and bred in Isfahan, and was the first of the family who came to Hindustan, where he was inrolled amongst the followers of Nawab Safdar Jang, the *wazir*. The father is called by another name in the Preface of this work, and in the *Miftahu-t Tawarikh* he is styled Muhammad Beg Khan.

Mirza Abu Talib was born at Lucknow, and was employed in posts of high emolument under Nawabs Shuja'u-d daula and Asafu-d daula. In the time of the latter he lost his office, and came to seek his subsistence from the English. By them he was hospitably entertained, and induced to visit Europe in 1799. He died and was buried at Lucknow in the year 1220 A.H. (1805 A.D.), as we learn from two chronograms composed by Beale at the request of Mirza Yusuf Bakir, the deceased's son, which are given at p. 564 of the *Miftahu-t Tawarikh*.

Besides the *Lubbu-s Siyar*, he wrote several other treatises, a Biography of the Poets, ancient and modern, and "himself indulged in versification, especially on the subject of the females of England, who aspire to equality with the Angels of Paradise, and he was always expatiating on the heart-ravishing strains of the women of that country, who used to sing at the public assemblies."[1]

CONTENTS

Preface, p. 1—Book I. On the Prophets, p. 2—II. On the events of the Khalifate, in seven chapters—Chap. i. The first four Khalifs, p. 9—ii. The Imams, p. 11—iii. The Ummayides, p. 12—iv. The 'Abbasides and their branches, p. 15—v. The Isma'ilians and their branches, p. 17—vi. The Saiyids, p. 19—vii. The Sharifs, p. 20—III. Biographies, in seven chapters—Chap. i. The Philosophers of Greece, Europe, India and Persia, and the moderns, p. 20—ii. The companions of the Prophet, p. 30—iii. The disciples, p. 31—iv. The religious teachers, p. 32—v. The learned men of Islam, p. 34—vi. The celebrated Poets, p. 37—vii. Other celebrated men of Islam, p. 38—IV. On the Sultans, in a Preface and eight Chapters—Preface on the climates, imaginary and real, and the old and new world, p. 39—Chap. i. The Sultans of Iran, including the Ghaznivides, Saljuks, Ghorians, etc., p. 45—ii. The Sultans of Arabia, p. 68—iii. The Sultans of Rum, p. 73—iv. The Rulers of Egypt and Syria, p. 76—v. The Kings of the West, p. 82—vi. The Sultans of Turkistan, p. 87—vii. The Kings of Europe, p. 101—viii. The Rulers of Hindustan, including the Hindu Rajas, the Kings of Dehli, of the Dakhin, Kashmir, and other independent kingdoms, p. 109.

This work is common in India. The best copy I have seen is in the possession of Razi-u-d din *Sadr-s Sudur* of Aligarh.

---

[1] *Zubdatu-l Gharaib*, 5th volume, v. Talib.

SIZE—Folio, 181 pages, each comprising 28 lines, closely written.

AUSAF-I ASAF

An historical sketch of the royal family of Oudh, written A.D. 1795. It is a useful work, containing also an account of contemporary princes.

SIZE—Large 8vo., 114 pages.

TARIKH
OF
JUGAL KISHWAR

This is a general history of India, by Jugal Kishwar, from the time of Humayun to Shah 'Alam. It is of no value, at least in the passages which I have examined. [Sir H. M. Elliot's library does not contain a copy of this work.]

GULISTAN-I RAHMAT
OF
NAWAB MUSTAJAB KHAN

This is a history of the Rohilla Afghans, and a life of Hafiz Rahmat Khan, written by his son Nawab Mustajab Khan Bahadur. The work has been abridged and translated by Charles Elliott. I have seen several histories of the Rohillas, but now none superior to this except the *Gul-i Rahmat* noticed in the next article.

The translator observes in his Introduction, "In the original many trivial occurrences are noticed which I have altogether omitted; and the repeated encomiums lavished by the Nawab upon the generosity and interpidity of his lamented parent, though honourable to his feelings as a son, would be deemed extravagant by the majority of readers, and indeed would scarcely admit of translation. A residence of many years in Rohilkhand, where the memory of Hafiz Rahmat Khan is held in the highest veneration, may perhaps have led me to attach a greater degree of importance to the work than it merits; but as Hafiz acted a distinguished part on the theatre of India for thirty years, and was personally engaged in every great action fought during that time, his life may furnish some materials to aid in the compliation of a history of that period; and with this view, I have taken considerable pains to correct some chronological errors in the original."

"It is necessary to add that Hamilton's History of the Rohillas will in some parts be found at variance with this narrative: that gentleman appears to have derived his information from the friends of the Nawab of Oudh, who would not be disposed to speak favourably of Hafiz Rahmat Khan, and as that work was published about the time of Hastings' trial, it might have been intended to frame an excuse for his permitting a British army to join on the attack in 1774 A.H."

GUL-I RAHMAT
OF
SA'ADAT YAR KHAN

The *Gul-i Rahmat* was written by Nawab Sa'adat Yar Khan, grandson of Hafiz Rahmat, and nephew of Mustajab Khan. It is more copious than the *Gulistan-i Rahmat*, though it professes to follow that work as its guide. It is divided into four parts: I. On the Genealogy of Hafiz Rahmat.—II. On 'Ali Muhammad Khan, and the arrival of Hafiz Rahmat in India.—III. Hafiz Rahmat Khan's administration of Katehr, and of the events which occurred there till the time of his death.— IV. Administration of Katehr under Shuja'u-d daula. Descendants of Hafiz Rahmat. This work was lithographed at Agra in 1836, in 221 small 8vo. pages of 17 lines each.

[The following Extracts have been selected and translated by the Editor. They will show how far this work differs from the *Gulistan-i Rahmat*, as translated by Elliot.]

EXTRACTS

[When Zabita Khan received intelligence of the passage (of the Ganges) by the Mahrattas, and of the deaths of Sa'adat Khan, Sadik Khan, and Karam Khan, the officers whom he had stationed to guard the ford, he was overpowered with astonishment, and fled in great bewilderment from Sakartal. He crossed the Ganges with a small escort, and proceeded to the camp of Faizu-llah Khan, carrying with him the intelligence of the Mahratta attack upon Najibabad. Faizu-llah Khan said: "I come here for the purpose of giving you advice; but as you will not listen to my words, I shall now go back to my own country." On hearing this declaration, Zabita Khan was still more downcast, and returned to his own forces. When he reached the Ganges, the good fortune of the Emperor plunged him into a sea of hesitation, and notwithstanding the number of his forces, and his powerful armament, he made no attempt to cross the river, but returned to Faizu-llah Khan.

When he arrived, he found Faizu-llah Khan seated on an elephant, about to depart. He mounted the same elephant, and proceeded with Faizu-llah to Rampur. On the news of his flight to Katchr reaching Sakartal, his soldiers were dispirited. They plundered each other, and then scattered in all directions. On receiving intelligence of these movements, the Mahrattas quickly advanced to Sakartal, and fell to plundering. . . . The garrison of the fort of Najibabad, who had held out in the hope of relief, were dismayed when they heard of the flight of Zabita Khan, and surrendered the fort to the royal forces. On taking possession of the fort, the people and family of Zabita Khan, including his son Ghulam Kadir, were placed in confinement. All the *materiel*, the treasure and the artillery collected by Najibu-d daula, fell into their hands.

On the news of the advance of the Mahrattas towards Rampur reaching the chiefs of Katehr, all the inhabitants of Anwala and Bisauli assembled. Fearing to be attacked by the Mahrattas, they fled in dismay to Bareilly. Some of them went to Pilibhit, intending to proceed to the hills. Hafiz Rahmat Khan[1] was returning from Farrukhabad to Tilhar when he heard of the defeat of Zabita Khan. He hastened to Bareilly, where he cheered and encouraged the chiefs and officers who were there assembled, and tried to dissuade them from removing to the hills. He said that the Mahrattas had no intention of attacking Katehr; and if they really did advance, negotiations might be opened with them and with the Emperor. If terms were agreed upon, all would be well; if not, they would fight. His auditors replied that there was no fortress of strength in Bareilly or Pilibhit: it was therefore desirable to carry off their families and property to the hills; for after these were placed in security, they themselves would be ready either for business or for war. Hafiz Rahmat reluctantly consented to their wishes. After Shaikh Kabir had entered Bareilly, Hafiz Rahmat took his departure, and leaving 'Inayat Khan in Pilibhit, he proceeded to Nanak-math, in the skirt of the hills. From thence he went with his followers and chiefs and soldiers to Gangapur, fiive *kos* distant in the hills, and surrounded with dense jungle, which secures it from the attacks of horsemen. There he remained. There also arrived Zabita Khan, in company with Faizu-llah Khan, who made their way through the jungle. Zabita Khan remained at Gangpur four days. He then found that Shuja'u-d daula was encamped at Shahabad, having advanced to the borders of his territories on hearing of the Maharatta attack upon Katehr.

[1]*He is generally entitled "Hafizu-l Mulk" in this work.*

Zabita Khan went off in great distress from Gangpur to see Shuja'u-d daula, and to solicit his assistance in obtaining the release of his family. After talking over the matter, Shuja'u-d daula postponed any action until after the arrival of Hafiz Rahmat. Zabita Khan wrote repeatedly to Hafiz Rahmat, begging him to come quickly. . . . The chiefs of Katehr suffered much from the inclemency of the climate of Gangpur, and yielding to their solicitations, Hafiz Rahmat proceeded quickly to Shahabad, at the beginning of the year 1186 A.H. (1772 A.D.), with three or four thousand men, horse and foot. When he approached, Shuja'u-d daula and the General Sahib went forth to meet him and pay him due respect.

After they had sat down together, they talked about the release of Zabita Khan's family, and of the settlement of his affairs with the Mahrattas. After much debate, Shuja'u-d daula and the General Sahib sent their *wakils* with some officers of Hafiz Rahmat to the Mahratta *sardars*. A great deal was said at the interview; but at length the Mahrattas sent a message to the effect that they would not give up the family of Zabita Khan until this sum of money was paid, nor would they loosen their hold upon his territory or the country of Katehr. The *wakils* had several meetings, and the Mahrattas at length agreed to take forty *lacs;* but they demanded as security for payment a deed under the seal of Shauja'u-d daula. The Nawab said that he had entered upon the matter entirely out of regard to Hafiz Rahmat, and that if Hfiz would give a bond for the pyament of the money, he would send his own bond to the Mahratta *sardars*. All the chiefs of Katehr who were present at the Council besought Hafiz Rahmat that he would without hesitation give his bond to Shuja'u-d daula, to secure peace for Zabita Khan, and said that they would all assist in the payment of the money. So Hafiz Rahmat, to befriend Zabita Khan, and to gratify the chiefs of Katehr, gave his bond for forty *lacs* of rupees to Shuja'u-d daula. The latter then executed his bond, and sent it to the Mahrattas.

In this he undertook to pay them forty *lacs* of rupees, when they had retired over the Jumna and entered Shah-Jahanabad, and when they had sent back the family of Zabita Khan, and had withdrawn their hands from the country of Katehr.

On receipt of this document, the Mahrattas sent the family of Zabita Khan to Shuja'u-d daula and Hafiz Rahmat; they then crossed the Ganges and proceeded towards Shah-Jahanabad. . . . When Hafiz Rahmat heard that Zabita Khan's family had reached Bareilly, he took leave of Shuja'u-d daula and General Parker, and went to Pilibhit. . . . After some days, Hafiz Rahmat called upon the chiefs of Katehr for the money he had become responsible for at their solicitation, and for which he had given his bond to Shuja'-d daula. They all began to lament their destitute condition, and made all sorts of excuses and evasions. Unable to do what he wished, Hafiz Rahmat did what he could, and sent the sum of five *lacs* out of his own treasury to Shuj'au-d daula. . . .

The *wakils* of Mahaji Sindhia and Taku Holkar, chiefs of the Mahrattas, waited upon Hafiz Rahmat, and informed him that their chiefs were about to attack the territories of Shuja'u-u daula, and that if he would join them, he should receive half of whatever territory should be conquered. If he declined to join them, they would respect his country, and return to him Shuja'u-d daula's bond for the forty *lacs* of rupees, no part of which had been paid, and give up all claim on that account, provided he would allow them a passage, and would make no opposition to their crossing the Ganges. In reply to these proposals, Hafi Rahmat requested time for consideration. Keeping the Mahratta *wakils* with him, he sent to inform Shuja'u-d daula of what the Mahrattas proposed, adding that they undertook to forego all claim upon himself for the forty *lacs* of rupees on condition of his remaining neutral. He added, "If you will send me back my sealed bond, and will hasten to oppose the

Mahrattas, I will dismiss the Mahratta *wakils*, and will guard the fords of the Ganges. United, we will beat the Mahrattas, and drive them from this country." Upon receipt of this letter, Shuja'u-d daula immediately wrote a reply (*expressing his gratification*), adding that he sent Saiyid Shah Madan as his representative, and that he would not deviate a hair's breadth from any agreement the Saiyid should make.... After his arrival, the Saiyid promised Hafiz Rahmat that the bond should be returned to him after the repulse of the Mahrattas, when he and Shuja'u-d daula would soon meet. The Nawab entreated Hafiz Rahmat to banish all suspicion, for there was no cause of dissension between them....

Hafiz Rahmat sent back the *wakils* with a proper answer to Shuja'u-d daula. On the same day he sent Ahmad Khan, son of the *Bakhshi*, in all haste from Anwala to secure the ford of Ram-ghat. A few days afterwards, hearing of the approach of the Mahrattas, he marched from Bareilly by way of Anwala to Bisauli. From that place he sent back the *wakils* of the Mahrattas, rejecting their proposals. He then proceeded with his small force to Ram-ghat. When the Mahratta *wakils* returned, they informed their chiefs of the little support given to Hafiz Rahmat, and of the smallness of his force. Hafiz Rahmat advanced to the distance of three *kos* from Asadpur, where Ahmad Khan was encamped, and in consequence of the celerity of his march his whole force had not come up: he had with him only four or five thousand men, horse and foot. The Mahrattas had received information through their spies of the limited number of his men, and resolved to attack him. They crossed the river during the night, and pressed onwards; but during the darkness they lost their way, and came upon Ahmad Khan's force, which they attacked. The pickets which Ahmad Khan had thrown out were watchful, and upon their reports the men were posted in the buildings and gardens of Asadpur. The fight raged hotly all day from morn till eve, and notwithstanding the immense numbers of the Mahrattas, they were unable to prevail over the small body of Afghans. After many men had been slain on both sides, Ahmad Khan, considering the immense force arrayed against him, sent a message to Taku Holkar and Sindhia, proposing an interview. They were only too glad to accede. Ahmad Khan went with a few followers to meet them. The Mahratta *sardars* kept him with them, and pitched their camp there.

The intelligence reached Hafiz Rahmat, while he was encamped near Asadpur, that 60,000 Mahrattas had crossed the river, and had attacked Ahmad Khan. He instantly drew out his forces, and was about to march for the relief of Ahmad Khan; but just then the news came that the Khan had gone to see the Mahratta chiefs. Hafiz Rahmat's chiefs and officers now urged upon him that it was inexpedient with his small force to wage war against the Mahratta hosts. . . . Muhibbu-llah Khan joined him with two or three thousand men, and Mustakin Khan also arrived with four or five thousand more; some others also came in, so that he now mustered ten or twelve thousand men. In the morning Hafiz Rahmat gave orders for the mustering of his forces to attack the Mahrattas, and all were in readiness, awaiting further orders, when messengers arrived from Shuja'd daula, announcing that his army was close at hand. As soon as he heard this, Hafiz Rahmat marched to attack the Mahrattas. At the same time the advanced forces of Shuja'u-d daula, General Chamkin (Champion) and Mahbub 'Ali Khan eunuch, came up at the critical moment, and opened fire with their guns upon the Mahrattas.

The forces of the Mahrattas were in two divisions. Mahaji Sindhia opposed Shuja'u-d daula, and Taku Holkar attacked Hafiz Rahmat. Both bodies of Mahrattas fought well and bravely; but the heavy fire of the English artillery and the flashing swords of the Afghans made them recede, and they took to flight

10.

Mahaji Sindhia passed over the Ganges by a bridge of boats, and halted on the other side. Taku Holkar was too hard pressed by the Afghans to be able to cross; so he fled on the same side of the river towards Sambhal. General Chamkin (Champion) and Mahbub 'Ali Khan crossed the river in their boats and attacked Sindhia, when he precipitately abandoned his baggage and camp, and took to flight, never stopping till he had covered five *kos*. The General seized upon his camp, took everything he found, and pitched his own camp upon the spot.

Hafiz Rahmat pursued Holkar for some distance; but the Mahrattas were mounted on swift horses, and traversed a long distance in the night. Hafiz Rahmat stopped near the battlefield to rest his men; Holkar went nearly to Sambhal, and he sent forward his advanced forces to plunder that place, and Muradabad and Rampur. . . . Hafiz Rahmat followed with all his force, and when Holkar heard of his near approach, he gave up his design upon Rampur, and fled in great disorder from Sambhal towards the ford of Phaphu. He reached the Ganges, and having crossed it with great exertion by swimming, he united his force with that of Sindhia. When Hafiz Rahmat heard of his having crossed and effected a junction with Sindhia, he proceeded towards Phaphu, and encamped upon the bank of the river. Afterwards he marched to join Shuja'u-d daula, who was encamped twelve *kos* off in face of Sindhia, to consult with him about the release of Ahmad Khan. After much parley Sindhia agreed to release his prisoner for a ransom of two *lacs* of rupees; and on payment of the money, Ahmad Khan obtained his liberty. Sindhia then marched off towards Dehli; Hafiz Rahmat and Shuja'u-d daula, by way of precaution, remained some days at the same place, and the two had frequent interviews.

Hafiz Rahmat sent Muhammad Khan and 'Abdu-llah Khan . . . to require from Shuja'u-d daula the return of the bond for forty *lacs*, in accordance with the verbal promise made by Shah Madan, his *wakil*. Shuja'u-d daula denied that he had ever made any promise to return it, and that Shah Madan could never have made such an offer. Hafiz Rahmat's friends urged that Shuja'u-d daula had written a letter promising to faithfully adhere to the verbal arrangements made by Shah Madan. They then required that Shah Madan should be brought forward, that he might be questioned upon the point. Shuja'u-d daula sent for him, and after trying to bias him, asked what it was that he had said to Hafiz Rahmat about the bond. Shah Madan was one of the honourable Saiyids of Shahabad, and deeming a lie to be derogatory to his honour, he spoke the whole truth, and nothing but the truth, saying, "In accordance with the directions of His Highness, I made a promise for the restoration of the bond." Shuja'u-d daula got into a rage, and said it was all a lie and a conspiracy, for he had never uttered a word of such a promise. Shah Madan three or four times affirmed the truth of his statement, and then held his peace. Khan Muhammad, seeing no hope of obtaining the bond, uttered some sharp words, at which Shuja'u-d daula also waxed warm, and went into his private apartments in a rage. Hafiz Rahmat did not deem it advisable to press further for the restoration of the bond at that time, and, concealing his annoyance, he said no more about it. Shuja'u-d daula was very much vexed with Hafiz Rahmat. He remained several days at the same place, and busied himself in winning over Hafiz Rahmat's officers and soldiers. . . .

At the end of the year 1187 A.H. (1773 A.D.), Shuja'u-d daula busied himself in winning over to his side, by various inducements, the people of Katehr, both small and great. . . . Having gained several chiefs and officers of that country, he felt full confidence, and marched to effect first the conquest of Etawa. The Mahratta detachments, which had been left there when their armies returned to the Dakhin, were too small in numbers to offer any resistance, and retreated before him. He soon made himself master of Etawa, and prepared to settle its administration. But Hafiz Rahmat wrote to him, protesting against this, and saying that the country of Etawa had been conferred upon him, after the battle of Panipat, by Ahmad Shah Durrani, as the Nawab knew full well. That after the end of the war, he had obtained possession of a large portion of the country, and although circumstances had made it necessary for him to allow the land to pass into the hands of the Mahrattas, he was about to take measures for recovering it. . . . Shuja'u-d daula wrote in answer that he had not taken the country from Hafiz Rahmat, but from the Mahrattas, so there was no cause of complaint. . . . Hafiz Rahmat repeatedly urged the restoration of Etawa; but Shuja'u-d daula, having secured the support of the chiefs of Katehr, was desirous of bringing the question to the test of war. So he wrote to Hafiz Rahmat, demanding speedy payment of the thirty-five *lacs* of rupees, which were due out of the forty thousand for which he (Shuja'u-d daula) had given his bond to the Mahrattas. After this had been settled, the question of Etawa might be gone into. After this, Shuja'u-d daula called together his forces, and prepared to march into Katehr.

Hafiz Rahmat, seeing that Shuja'u-d daula was intent upon war, wrote in reply, "The money which the Mahrattas received from you has already been rapid; to demand more from me than the Mahrattas have either received or asked, and to make it the excuse for strife and warfare, is unworthy of your high position. If, in spite of everything, you are resolved upon war, I am ready for you." On receipt of this letter, the Nawab drew together his forces, and prepared to pass the Ganges by way of Koriya-ganj. Hafiz Rahmat also ordered his camp to be pitched outside of the town on the Anwala side.

General Champion, who was with Shuja'u-d daula, wrote to Hafiz Rahmat, promising that, if he would pay the money, or would promise to pay it in two or three months, he (the General) would, by his own influence, effect a peace, and cause Shuja'u-d daula to return to his own country. Pahar Singh, *diwan* of Katehr, [*urged Hafiz Rahmat to assent to the General's advice*]. But death had deprived him of all his friends and supporters, such as . . . , and especially of 'Inayat Khan, his son; he had therefore withdrawn his heart from the world, and was desirous of martyrdom. He said that he had not got the money, or he would send it; and that to ask others for it, to seize it by force, or to be under any obligation to Shuja'u-d daula for it, he considered so disgraceful, that he would leave the matter to the arbitrament of God, and would welcome martyrdom. . . . He sent an answer to the General to the above effect. Then he issued a general order in these words, "Let those who think fit accompany me, and let those who are unwilling depart. Each man may do as he likes. I have many enemies and few friends, but this I heed not."

On the 11th Muharram, 1188 A.H. (24th March, 1774 A.D.), Hafiz Rahmat marched out of Bareilly with a moderate force, and went towards Anwala. . . . The alarm of war having spread, numbers of Afghans from Mau and Farrukhabad, and the inhabitants of Katehr, both subjects and strangers, obeying the instinct of clanship, gathered round Hafiz Rahmat. *Zamindars* of the *Rajput* tribe, who had lived in peace under his rule, came in troops to support him without summons, so that his army increased in numbers every day. . . . Hafiz Rahmat marched from Tanda, and crossing the Ramganga at the ford of Kiyara, he entered Faridpur, seven *kos* to the east of Bareilly. Shuja'u-d daula advanced by successive marches to Shah-Jahanpur. . . . From thence he went on to Tilhar, where he rested and prepared for action. Hafiz Rahmat then marched from Faridpur, and crossing the river Bhagal, encamped in the groves around Karra. There was then a distance of not more than seven or eight *kos* between the two armies. . . .

Two or three days after, Shupa'u-d daula, acting on

the advice of General Champion, who was the most accomplished General of the time, made a march towards Pilibhit, and halted at the village of Musali, where there was a wide open plain. Reports of an intended attack on Pilibhit spread through both armies. Hafiz Rahmat thereupon left Karra, for the purpose of protecting Pilibhit, and encamped in face of the enemy in the open plain. . . . General Champion cheered the drooping heart of Shuja'u-d daula and taking the command of the advanced force, he selected the positions for the guns, and made the necessary arrangements for the battle. . . .

On the 11th Safar Shuja'u-d daula advanced with an army numbering 115,000 horse and foot. . . Hafiz Rahmat went to the tent of Faizu-llah Khan, and said, "My end is near at hand. So long as I remain alive, do not turn away from the field; but when I fall, beware, do not press the battle, but leave the field directly, and flee with my children and dependents to the hills. This is the best course for you to take, and if you act upon my advice, it will be the better for you." After giving those directions, he mounted his horse, and marched against the enemy with ten thousand horse and foot. He had proceeded only a short distance, when the advanced force of the enemy came in sight, and fire was opened from cannons and muskets. . . . Ahmad Khan, son of the *Bakhshi*, who had made a secret agreement with Shuja u-d daula, now fell back, and set the example of flight, which many others followed. . . Hafiz Rahmat had only about fifty supporters left when he drew near to the Telingas and English. He was recognized by his umbrella, of which spies had given a description, and a cannon was levelled against him. He advanced in front of all his companions, using his utmost efforts. The canon-balls fell all around, and . . . at length one struck him on the breast. He was lifted off his horse, and after taking a sip or two of water, he drank the cup of martyrdom.

SHAH-NAMA
OR
MUNAWWARU-L KALAM
OF
SHEO DAS

[This compilation commences with the reign of Farrukh Siyar, and ends with the fourth year of the reign of Muhammad Shah, but it was not finished before the year 1217 A.H. (1802 A.D). The author was Sheo Das, of Lucknow. He was moved to write the work by the consideration that "he had been allowed to remain a long time in the society of learned, scientific, and highly talented men—and had spent his life in the service of the great. He had moreover applied himself to acquiring the art of writing with elegance, and so he determined to show the results of his society in his composition. He named his work *Shah-nama* or *Munawwaru-l Kalam*, because he had been on terms of intimacy with the great, and derived advantages from them." He follows the fashion of historians, and, although a Hindu, opens his work like a devout Musulman.

The whole of this work has been translated for Sir H. M. Elliot by "Lieut. Prichard, 15th Regt. N. I." The work contains a good deal of biography and anecdote, but the period it covers has been already provided for by Extracts from contemporary writers.]

IKHTISARU-T TAWARIKH
OF
SAWAN SINGH

THIS compendium was composed in the year 1217 A.H. (1802 A.D.) by Sawan Singh, son of Than Singh, a Kayath of the Mathur tribe. It is professedly a mere abridgment of the *Lubbu-t Tawarikh* of Bhara Mal, and the *Hadikatu-t Akalim*.

CONTENTS

Preface, p. 1—Hindu Rajas, p. 8—Musulman Kings of Dehli; Muhammad Sam to Babar, p. 16—Babar, Afghans, and Humayun, p. 73—Akbar and Jahangir, p. 96—Shah Jahan and Aurangzeb, p. 98—Shah 'Alam I. to Shah 'Alam II., p. 148.

Size 8vo. 181 pages, each containing 16 lines.

The *Ikhtisaru-t Tawarikh* contains nothing worth translation.

The only copy I have seen of this work is in the possession of Maulavi Subhan 'Ali, of Amroha, in the district of Muradabad.

THE END

www.ingramcontent.com/pod-product-compliance
Lightning Source LLC
Chambersburg PA
CBHW030309170426
43202CB00009B/925